Cambridge Elements ⦀

Elements in the Philosophy of Martin Heidegger
edited by
Filippo Casati
Lehigh University
Daniel O. Dahlstrom
Boston University

HEIDEGGER ON POETIC THINKING

Charles Bambach
University of Texas at Dallas

CAMBRIDGE
UNIVERSITY PRESS

Shaftesbury Road, Cambridge CB2 8EA, United Kingdom

One Liberty Plaza, 20th Floor, New York, NY 10006, USA

477 Williamstown Road, Port Melbourne, VIC 3207, Australia

314–321, 3rd Floor, Plot 3, Splendor Forum, Jasola District Centre, New Delhi – 110025, India

103 Penang Road, #05–06/07, Visioncrest Commercial, Singapore 238467

Cambridge University Press is part of Cambridge University Press & Assessment, a department of the University of Cambridge.

We share the University's mission to contribute to society through the pursuit of education, learning and research at the highest international levels of excellence.

www.cambridge.org
Information on this title: www.cambridge.org/9781009570572

DOI: 10.1017/9781009570565

First published 2024

A catalogue record for this publication is available from the British Library

ISBN 978-1-009-57057-2 Hardback
ISBN 978-1-009-57055-8 Paperback
ISSN 2976-5668 (online)
ISSN 2976-565X (print)

Cambridge University Press & Assessment has no responsibility for the persistence or accuracy of URLs for external or third-party internet websites referred to in this publication and does not guarantee that any content on such websites is, or will remain, accurate or appropriate.

Heidegger on Poetic Thinking

Elements in the Philosophy of Martin Heidegger

DOI: 10.1017/9781009570565
First published online: November 2024

Charles Bambach
University of Texas at Dallas

Author for correspondence: Charles Bambach,cbambach@utdallas.edu

Abstract: One of the striking features of Heidegger's philosophical engagement concerns his privileging of poetry and poetic thinking. In this understanding of language as fundamentally poetic, Heidegger puts forward a different way to do philosophy. In this Element, Heidegger's poetic thinking is placed in conversation with Sophocles and Hölderlin as a way to situate his critique of global technology and instrumental thinking in the postwar years. This Element also offers a critique of Heidegger's efforts to arrogate poetic thinking to his own aim of a destinal form of German national self-assertion through poetry. Overall, the aim here is to show how crucial poetic thinking is to the way Heidegger understands philosophy as a radical engagement with language.

Keywords: poetry, dwelling, ethics, Heidegger, thinking

ISBNs: 9781009570572 (HB), 9781009570558 (PB), 9781009570565 (OC)
ISSNs: 2976-5668 (online), 2976-565X (print)

Contents

Introduction

As a discourse that involves a discursive turn back to its own foundations, philosophy has to do with thinking. And yet for Martin Heidegger, it is precisely in the realm of philosophy that such thinking comes to us as impoverished, marked by the deficit of its own self-scrutiny. As Heidegger contends, what is most thought-provoking in our thought-provoking time is that we are still not yet thinking (GA 8: 6). To address such a deficit, Heidegger will offer a critique of traditional philosophical thinking by turning to poets and poetry in an effort to initiate a leap into an other form of thinking, one deeply attuned to the poetic character of language. In this Cambridge Element on Heidegger's poetic thinking, we will address his readings of poetic texts and explore the meaning of his turn to Greek tragedy as a way of negotiating his concerns about history, nationality, and the experience of the foreign that he holds is essential for grasping our own native identity. Perhaps foremost of our concerns here will be a focus on the way Heidegger privileges the poetry of Hölderlin for coming to understand language as a way of opening a different approach to thinking than the one traditionally embraced by philosophers. As we will see, the name "Hölderlin" will become for Heidegger synonymous with the effort to "think" otherwise than the tradition of Western thinking, as it offers a pathway out of metaphysics, serving as "the harbinger of the overcoming of metaphysics" (GA 52: 143/HHR: 122). As a philosopher skeptical of the metaphysical incursions of the discipline of philosophy, Heidegger will come to call for "the end of philosophy," by which he means "the completion of metaphysics in the unconditional forgetting of being (nihilism) that is the neglect or unguarding (*Verwahrlosung*) of beyng" (GA 97: 480). As Heidegger sees it, contemporary philosophy has come to mean a way of thinking about beings in the manner of a representational thinking that provides grounds. Under the dominance of the sciences, our current thinking "will soon be determined and regulated by the new fundamental science called cybernetics" (GA 14: 72). Here, with the rise of globalization that arranges, parcels, distributes, regulates, plans, and directs human commerce and consumption, the hegemony of calculative thinking gains such a foothold that it begins to be taken for granted as the only legitimate form of thinking. As Heidegger phrases it: "The end of philosophy shows itself as the triumph of the steerable arrangement of a scientific-technological world and of the social order in compliance with this world. The end of philosophy means: the beginning (*Beginn*) of the world civilization grounded in Western European thinking" (GA 14: 73).

Given the omnipresence of this kind of technological-scientific form of thinking, Heidegger asks whether its historical predominance will one day emerge as "the sole measure of the human being's sojourn in the world?" (GA 14: 75). As he negotiates the terrain of modern philosophical thinking, Heidegger identifies a long series of philosophical habits and practices that serve to block or occlude a pathway into the genuine experience of thinking. The upshot of Heidegger's determination of the end of philosophy is to show how the metaphysical thinking of modernity – secured in a tendentious reading of the first Greek beginning – has contributed to the oblivion of being. At the same time, in his overarching scheme of the history of being, he reminds us that this epochal situation belongs essentially to the self-veiling essence of being and not merely to human initiatives or deficiencies (GA 5: 364–365). Forgetfulness and oblivion are written into the very grammar of being's lexicon. The challenge is, however, to approach this most concealed of all concealments in a way that preserves its veiled character without seeking to render it clear and comprehensible. If we follow the logic of machination, we then turn toward ameliorating this deficit by redirecting our attention to the management and manipulation of beings. Such a course has the inevitable effect of re-inscribing the very nihilism that such oblivion has brought with it. Yet Heidegger does not retreat into a revised mode of Schopenhaueran pessimism. Instead, he offers an alternative to the computational thinking that has entrenched our epoch in precisely the kind of oblivion that it fails to recognize. Against such oblivion, Heidegger attempts a different way of thinking, one attuned to remembrance, commemoration, and poetic recollection; a thinking or *Denken* that is ever bound to *Andenken*. By thinking of *Andenken* as a commemorative thinking, Heidegger does not think it simply as "remembrance," "the mere making present of something past" (GA 4: 96). Rather, *Andenken* in Heidegger's sense is turned toward the future in a way that thinks (*denkt*) ahead toward (*an-*) that which is coming. Hence, Heidegger can write: "because this thinking thinks in the manner of remembrance (*andenkend denkt*) and never merely represents something at hand, it must at the same time think in the direction of that which is coming" (GA 52: 165/HHR: 140). For Heidegger, *Andenken* needs to be experienced as "a recollective thinking ahead" (GA 71: 313/E: 272).

Such a form of thinking cannot follow the prescribed rules of thinking laid out in logic or metaphysics that always privileges presence over absence, ground over abyss (*Grund, Abgrund*), representation over imagination, and calculation over meditation. This other form of thinking, a thinking that essays to think being without reducing it to beings, requires a leap (*Sprung*) into being, "a leap into the groundless from the habitual ground upon which for us, in each case, beings are" (GA 54: 223). This leap into being cannot take place, however, if our starting point remains beings as such (GA 70: 110). What is required here is a different kind of thinking, what Heidegger will come to call a "poetic thinking" that, as preparatory thinking, thinks "the preparation of the inceptivity of the other beginning" (GA 70: 56). This form of thinking constitutes what Heidegger names an *Absprung* or a "leap of departure" apart from metaphysics and into the preparation for an other beginning, one whose possibility Heidegger links to poetry, more particularly, the poetry of Hölderlin. For Heidegger: "Such thinking prepares a poetizing that, in Hölderlin's hymns, has already taken place, that is, essentially prevails in a genuinely inceptive sense (*echt anfänglich west*)" (GA 70: 156). As Heidegger sees it, Hölderlin's poetizing "has left metaphysics behind" with its leap since its way of engaging language points us toward "the founding of being in the word" (GA 4: 41).

What Hölderlin points the way toward is an experience of "the intimacy of the inception in its other inceptivity" (*die Innigkeit des Anfangs in seiner anderen Anfänglichkeit*) (GA 70: 159). In this sense, Hölderlin becomes for Heidegger "the poet of the other beginning" (GA 70: 160). But Hölderlin's poetic work does not itself constitute a way of "thinking," since poetry resists being transformed into a form of thinking or converted into concepts. Between poetizing and thinking (*Dichten und Denken*), Heidegger maintains, "there always remains a chasm, for they 'dwell on the most separate mountains'" (GA 11: 26; DKV I: 350). In "On the Essence of Language," Heidegger returns to his distinction between poetizing and thinking and underscores how it is a rip or tear (*Riss*) that obtains between them, one that "tears poetizing and thinking open to one another in a relation of nearness . . . The nearness that nears is itself the appropriating event (*Ereignis*) out of which poetizing and thinking are referred to the proper (*Eigene*) of their essence" (GA 12: 185). Poetizing and thinking are indeed marked "by a fragile yet luminous difference," Heidegger admits, even as they share "a concealed affinity" that holds sway in the way each "employs and squanders itself in service to language for language's sake" (GA 11: 26). But poetry is in no way subordinate to language, as if it were a mere handmaiden in service to some form of language beyond itself. For Heidegger reminds us "poetry never takes language as a raw material present at hand; rather, poetry itself first makes language possible" (GA 4: 43). Thus, Heidegger claims, "the essence of language must be understood out of the essence of poetry and not the other way around." In order to properly grasp the preeminence of poetizing here – especially in an age overdetermined by a nonpoetic, calculative form of thinking – requires of us a wholly different approach to thinking the history of Western thinking in the early Greeks. Here the poetic influence of Hölderlin becomes determinative. For what Hölderlin's radical approach to language opens up for Heidegger is in providing the push for a possible leap into an other beginning by way of resituating us in our relation to the first Greek beginning. For "in Hölderlin's poetry there waits for us the possibility of an other manifestation of beyng" (GA 75: 81). It is in Hölderlin's poetic word – in conversation with Heraclitus – that "that understanding of beyng that came to power at the beginning of Western philosophy lies near and is once again powerful" (GA 39: 123). What comes to notice here is the way Hölderlin's role proves decisive for Heidegger.

Apart from his singular status as "poet of the Germans," "poet of poets," and "the poet – that is, the founder – of German beyng," Hölderlin stands for Heidegger as the one figure who takes on "the task of the thoughtful meditation on the first beginning – and that means on the other, futural beginning of Western thinking" (GA 39: 214, 220; GA 45: 135). It is in this sense that Heidegger can nominate Hölderlin as "the poet of the other beginning of our futural history" (GA 66: 426). Heidegger's lifelong engagement with Hölderlin and with his poetic language helps to open for him a possibility of thinking that attempts a way of engaging being that does not draw upon the thinking of metaphysics. In attempting this kind of poetic thinking, Heidegger seeks to prepare the way for an other beginning for thinking. This initiative does not leave behind the first Greek beginning, but attempts to retrieve what remains unthought in that beginning as a way to energize the leap into the other beginning.

As we turn our attention in this Element to a fuller appraisal of Heidegger's poetic thinking, we will look at how Heidegger's relationship to the Greeks (by way of Hölderlin) will come to shape his understanding of technology, instrumental thinking, language, the earth, the homeland, *Gelassenheit*, and poetic dwelling.

1 Hölderlin Between the First and the Other Beginning

1.1 What Are Poets For?

In an essay from December 1946 celebrating the twentieth anniversary of Rilke's death, Heidegger addresses the question about the vocation and task of the poet in "a destitute time" (GA 5: 221/OBT: 202). Drawing on the Hölderlinian conceit of "the gods that have fled" ("Bread and Wine," v. 147), Heidegger sees his own time as "the time of the world's night," the time where human beings stand abandoned in a world of desolation. Enduring a world marked by "the default of God" (*der Fehl Gottes*), the human being comes to recognize that "the radiance of divinity is extinguished in world-history" (GA 5: 269/OBT: 200). Hölderlin poignantly expresses this plight of human destitution in his ode, "The Gods," where he writes:

> You dear gods, he who does not know you is impoverished,
> In his raw heart dissonance never comes to rest,
> And the world is night for him and no
> Joy flourishes for him and no song. (DKV I: 243)

Such a state of loss comes to word at the very end of another ode of Hölderlin's, "The Poet's Vocation," where the situation is reminiscent of the poet's lament for the flight of the gods in his famous elegy "Bread and Wine" (vv. 115–116). There Hölderlin poetizes the vocation of the poet as one who must stand alone if the help of others does not keep away the darkness of night and where he must wait, in his simplicity, "until the default of God helps" (DKV I: 307). For Heidegger, these poetic utterances come to play an inordinately crucial role in the way he negotiates the terrain of the late modern landscape. Philosophizing in the epochal situation of "the death of god," Heidegger turns to Hölderlin's language as a way of grasping the proper role of "thinking" as an alternative to the academic profession of philosophy. Heidegger finds in a conversation with Hölderlin the outline of a timely form of "poetic thinking" that he had already called for in his early Black Notebooks.

In what follows, I want to offer a reading of Heidegger's poetic thinking as a way to explore his reflection on the distress of the modern age. In his 1951 essay "Building Dwelling Thinking," Heidegger takes up this question as a way to reflect on the meaning of poetic dwelling. As Karsten Harries has reminded us, this essay was originally presented at an exhibition commemorating the artist colony in Darmstadt from 1901.[1] The preamble that accompanied this exhibition announced itself as a response to "the age of technology," which was characterized by the awareness that "the plight of our age is homelessness." Yet Heidegger does not take this question of homelessness at face value. Writing in 1951 in the midst of the postwar housing shortage brought on by the Allied bombing of German cities, Heidegger emphasizes that our homelessness does not reside in our lack of proper housing that could be overcome by constructing better urban residences. Nor is it a matter of improved drafting methods or architectural expertise. As Heidegger writes:

> ... the authentic plight of dwelling does not consist first of all in the lack of residences. The authentic plight of dwelling is indeed older than the world wars and their destruction, older also than the rise of native populations upon the earth and the circumstances of industrial workers. The authentic plight of dwelling rests in this, that mortals search ever anew for the essence of dwelling, that they *must first learn what dwelling is*. What if the homelessness of the human being were to consist in this – that the human being still does not even ponder (*bedenken*) the *authentic* plight of dwelling *as the* plight? As soon as the human being *ponders* this homelessness, however, it is no longer a misery. Properly pondered and well-remembered, it is the sole summons that *calls* mortals into dwelling. (GA 7: 163–164/PLT: 161 tm)

---

[1] Karsten Harries, "In Search of Home," in Eduard Fuhr, ed., *Bauen und Wohnen/Building and Dwelling: Martin Heidegger's Foundation of a Phenomenology of Architecture* (Münster: Waxmann, 2000), 101–120.

This sense of dwelling for Heidegger is intimately tied to the work of Hölderlin, especially his late poem "In lovely blueness . . .," where the poet reflects on the relation of mortals and gods set against the tension between sky and earth. There the poet asks:

> Is God unknown? Is he manifest as the sky? I'd sooner believe this. Of the human, measure it is. Full with what is our due, yet poetically, dwells the human being on this earth. (DKV I: 479)

For Heidegger, Hölderlin's poetizing of human dwelling remains one of the most pressing concerns for his entire thought path. Moreover, such a concern comes to shape not merely questions about poetry, dwelling, habitation, or lodging, but the very sense and meaning of human existence, what philosophers have traditionally defined as questions of "ethics." As we shall see, Heidegger will often understand the discourse of traditional ethics as an enterprise entangled in the calculative rationality of planning, regulation, and rulemaking. Yet for Heidegger, ethics, in its originary sense, has less to do with rules and methods than it does with the simple sense of dwelling. Much as he deconstructs modern physics back to its roots in ancient Greek *physis* and logic back to the Heraclitean understanding of ancient *logos*, Heidegger will rethink modern calculative ethics in terms of the early Greek understanding of *ethos*. As he thinks it, "*ethos* means dwelling (*Wohnung*), sojourn (*Aufenthalt*). We say: the dwelling of the human being, its sojourn in the midst of beings as a whole" (GA 55: 214/H: 162). In his Heraclitus lectures from SS 1944, Heidegger goes on to explain that

> Originally, *ethos* means dwelling, sojourn . . . The understanding of *ethos*, the knowledge of it, is 'ethics.' Here we take this word in a very broad and essential sense. The conventional meaning of ethics as a moral doctrine, a theory of virtue, or even a doctrine of values, is merely the consequence, mutation, and aberration of the concealed originary meaning. . . . *To ethos* is the comportment (*Haltung*) of the human being's sojourn (*Aufenthalt*) in the midst of beings as a whole. (GA 55: 206–207/H: 156–157)

Those of us who read Heidegger sometimes forget that the question of ethical dwelling does not begin in the postwar works of the late Heidegger or even with the onset of the Hölderlin lectures in WS 1934–1935, even if there it receives a new emphasis. Rather, Heidegger's focus on *ethos* goes back to various readings of Aristotle in his early works. In SS 1924, Heidegger writes: "*Ethos* means the 'comportment' (*Haltung*) of the human being, how the human being is *there*, how he gives himself as a human being" (GA 18: 106). From these early lectures, two essential themes emerge that will come to define Heidegger's work on dwelling, sojourn, human comportment, and ethics. First, the fundamental stance of the human being, its *Haltung* or *ethos*, is not primarily "moral" but has, rather, to do with the way the human being holds itself open (*hält sich auf*) for the truth of being. Second, this comportment of the human being, its way of abiding, residing, sojourning in the world – in other words, its way of dwelling, its *ethos* – is profoundly connected with language. As Heidegger will see it, language is inseparably bound to our habitual haunts (*ethea*), our ways of abiding and dwelling, our *ethos*. Language is the authentic abode of the human being, that which grants to us our sense of belonging in the world to place, dialect, people, community, and historical destiny. Such dwelling and its poetic possibilities will, for Heidegger, be inextricably linked to the poetic language of Hölderlin.

We are inclined to ask: Why is poetry (*Dichtung*) so essential for Heidegger, especially in the way he approaches the task of thinking – and of thinking anew what calls for thinking? It is this question that animates this Cambridge Element on "Heidegger's Poetic Thinking." But before turning to a more considered approach to the question of poetic thinking, we should first reflect on the meaning of Heidegger's own terms. Perhaps the locus classicus for taking up this question is Heidegger's 1951 essay "... poetically dwells the human being ...," which we will look at in greater detail in a later section. We will also need to consider Heidegger's way of situating the question of *Dichtung* in regards to his discourse on the first and other beginning. Here we will need to take up the relation of poetry to Greek tragedy and especially Heidegger's reading of Sophocles' play *Antigone* to which he devotes two distinct texts: his 1935 lecture course *Introduction to Metaphysics* and the SS 1942 lecture *Hölderlin's Hymn, 'The Ister.'* Why, we might ask, does the *Gespräch* (conversation) between ancient Greek poetry and modern German poetry/thinking take on such inordinate significance for Heidegger? And what role does Hölderlin come to play within such a conversation? Moreover, how does this reading of Hölderlin and the Greeks come to shape Heidegger's postwar writings on technology, positionality (*Gestell*), and the role of language? These are some of the most essential questions in Heidegger's entire corpus and, I will argue, they remain part of Heidegger's lifelong conversation with Hölderlin, who comes to embody for the thinker of being, the richest expression of human dwelling within the tradition of Western thinkers and poets. We will need to look more closely at Heidegger's writings on Hölderlin within the context of his own thought path. This will involve us in needing to situate his readings of the poet within German history in all its brutality and furor.

For Heidegger, the very name Hölderlin will come to stand for a singular German experience of history in terms of a destinal politics of the Volk. Even the casual reader will by now have heard of the latest scandal concerning Heidegger's Black Notebooks with their "sensational" revelations about the author's Nazi commitments and anti-Semitic remarks.[2] We will need to address this underlying paradox in Heidegger's work between the poetic thinking of the human being and the earth *and* the undermining of "thinking" in Heidegger's political commitments to National Socialism and its attendant anti-Semitic tenets. As I read it, we cannot simply suppress these political commitments and then move on to serious philosophical discussion. There is something deeply unsettling about these texts that force us to confront our own contradictions as human beings. To simply condemn Heidegger and congratulate ourselves in so doing will hardly prove a worthy strategy. In this spirit, we need to address the brutal chiasm in Heidegger's thinking between the chauvinism that places the German Volk at the center of an exceptional historical destiny *and* the attention to poetic thinking that proffers an alternative to such exceptionalism. For what is remarkable in some of these same texts is Heidegger's commitment to a poetic *ethos* of dwelling that promulgates a "real revolution in our relationship to language" (GA 40: 57/IM: 58). In "... poetically dwells the human being ...," Heidegger writes that "the human being first speaks (*spricht*) only and insofar as it corresponds to language (*die Sprache entspricht*), in that it heeds its appeal (*Zuspruch*)" (GA 7: 194/PLT: 216 tm). But few human beings do indeed heed such an appeal, Heidegger tells us. Instead, we are inundated by the proliferation of "an unbridled, but dexterous talking and writing and broadcasting of the spoken word around the globe. The human being acts as if it were the sculptor and master of language even as language remains the master of the human being." Along with this global transformation of language into a tool for communication, commerce, and capital, there persist traces and hints of a different understanding and experience of language in the work of poets such as Hölderlin. In Hölderlin's poetic word, we learn how "poetizing first and foremost lets dwelling be dwelling. Poetizing is the proper letting-dwell" (GA 7: 193/PLT: 213).

Ultimately, what comes to question here for Heidegger in his discourse of poetic dwelling and thinking is nothing less than the fate of the earth and of the human being's place within the fourfold gathering that constitutes our epochal destiny. As a response to this crisis of dwelling, Heidegger calls for a fundamental revolution in ethics, a call for how *ethos* is more originary than the traditional metaphysical discourse of ethics rooted in values, judgments, and worldviews.

---

[2] The scholarship concerning Heidegger's political and racial comments in the Black Notebooks is still growing, but the most significant work includes books by Peter Trawny, *Heidegger und der Mythos der jüdischen Weltverschwörung* (Frankfurt: Klostermann, 2014); Andrew Mitchell & Peter Trawny, eds., *Heidegger's Black Notebooks: Responses to Anti-Semitism* (New York: Columbia University Press, 2017), and Jeff Malpas & Ingo Farin, eds., *Reading Heidegger's "Black Notebooks" 1931–1941* (Cambridge: MIT Press, 2015).

The danger that currently assails the human being "consists in the threat that bears upon the essence of the human being in its relationship to being . . . This danger is *the* danger (*Gefahr*). It conceals itself in the abyss that pervades all beings" (GA 5: 296/OBT: 222 tm). In order to recognize this abyssal danger, Heidegger claims, there must first be mortals capable of reaching into the abyss. In his 1803 hymn "Patmos," Hölderlin poetizes the plight of the modern age as an era in default, an age marked by the departure and flight of the gods. For him, this takes the form of a sacred mourning over the retreat of the divine from human history that leaves behind what the poet calls an "abyss" (*Abgrund*). Drawing on the image of Alpine valleys that separate distant peaks, Hölderlin envisions the task of the poet as one of crossing over the abyss between summits on fragile, "lightly built" bridges. But if the danger of the crossing appears too great, the poet responds with the hope of a salvific gesture. In verses that Heidegger will cite often, Hölderlin addresses this precarious state:

> Wo aber Gefahr ist, wächst / But where there is danger,
> Das Rettende auch. / There grows also that which saves. (DKV I: 350)[3]

In the age of atomic destruction and its ever-recurring threat, Heidegger will transform Hölderlin's poetic theology of *Übergang*, *Gefahr*, and *das Rettende* into a thinker's reflection on the danger of all dangers – the danger of not even recognizing the danger.[4] As the poet of the intimate relation between danger and that which saves, Hölderlin's word bespeaks the peril of reducing the poetic word to mere "interpretation." Heidegger's ways of reading Hölderlin reject the possibility of approaching him in terms of either "literary-historiological 'explications' or even 'philosophical interpolations.' Instead, they seek in Hölderlin's poetry a historical foothold that could prepare a creative thinking of the beginning. To be sure, what manifests itself there is a historical vocation of Hölderlin's poetry of which we still know nothing, since the essence of this history is still concealed to us" (GA 71: 336/E: 291 tm). Heidegger turns to Hölderlin, then, as the poet who, in a time of destitution, addresses the question – "Why Poets?" Living in the age of the world wars, Heidegger insists that the mere bankruptcy and destruction brought on by "a world catastrophe can so little lead into what is inceptual as the previous world wars" (GA 80: 1037). Before there can be anything like a turn from out of the darkness of the world's night, we need to cultivate an "ability to hear" the poetic word (GA 71: 335). Such a transformation requires time. As Hölderlin himself was to write in his hymn "Mnemosyne":

---

[3] See, for example, GA 79:72; GA 4: 21; GA 76:29; GA 5: 296.
[4] In the Bremen lectures, Heidegger writes: "The danger is the epoch of being essencing as positionality" (*Die Gefahr ist die Epoche des Seyns wesend als Gestell*) GA 79:70 BFL: 68.

Lang ist

Die Zeit, es ereignet sich aber
Das Wahre./

Long is

The time, yet the true
Comes to pass.

(DKV I: 1032)[5]

As Heidegger comes to reflect on the time required to cultivate the attunement required to hear the poet's word, he asks:

How much longer are we still going to resist experiencing beings as beings? How much longer do the Germans still want to turn a deaf ear to the word sung by Hölderlin in the first stanza of the "Patmos" hymn?

Near is
And difficult to grasp the god . . .
(GA 4: 21/EHP: 40 tm)

Given the current state of our unpreparedness to grasp what is nearest to us, Heidegger asks in a voice that is both poignant and filled with genuine urgency – "What can we then do to rescue the poem from out of its homelessness? Are we at all capable of freeing the poetic from its exile?" (GA 80: 1039). The symptoms of nihilism lie everywhere present in the postwar German landscape as Heidegger delivers his 1951 lecture "On Contemporary Poetry." Planetary devastation, the reign of calculative thinking, the unimpeded triumph of machination and/as positionality – all of these give testimony to the historical manifestation of the abandonment of being. Drawing on Hölderlin's poetic experience of both the flight of the gods and the lack of holy names, Heidegger offers his own reflections on the loss of our ability to *hear* the poetic word.

The poem is only still read by readers.
It no longer sings. (GA 80: 1039)

Despite these bleak tidings, Heidegger still can say:

And yet!
" . . . poetically dwells/The human being upon this earth . . ."

It is in terms of this possibility – and essential vocation – of the human being to dwell poetically upon the earth that Heidegger offers his own reading of Hölderlin. Yet to those who are intimately familiar with Germany's long and distinguished poetic tradition and to those who are not, the question becomes:

---

[5] Heidegger will cite these lines in a range of texts, here the most prominent include GA 5: 270; GA 39:55–56; GA 52: 180, and GA 97:70.

Why does Heidegger decide to nominate Hölderlin as the one poet capable of confronting our historical plight in an essential way?

2 Hölderlin and the Task of Poetic Thinking

2.1 Poetry and the Enigma of Ethical Life

In order to understand Heidegger's decision to nominate Hölderlin as his "mouthpiece" (*Sprachrohr*), we should start with his lecture course from WS 1934–1935 *Hölderlin's Hymns 'Germania' and 'The Rhine,'* the first of three courses Heidegger devoted to the poet. In April 1934, Heidegger decides to abandon his post as rector of Freiburg University and to return to full-time teaching. As he grapples with his own failure to help bring about a genuine revolution in thinking, following through the political revolution in German national identity achieved by National Socialism, Heidegger turns to Hölderlin. At this critical juncture, Heidegger abandons his ambition "to lead the Führer" (*den Führer führen*) and instead chooses a different path of engagement nourished on Hölderlin's still unacknowledged role as "the poet of the Germans" (GA 39: 214, 220/HGR: 195, 201).[6] For the next forty years, Hölderlin will come to occupy an essential place in Heidegger's thinking. Not only will Hölderlin accompany Heidegger through the numerous turns and inflections on his thought path, but he will open Heidegger to his concealed vocation of becoming the thinker of an other beginning for thinking. As Heidegger's student Hans-Georg Gadamer knew all too well, "Hölderlin's poetic work accompanied Heidegger as an enduring source of orientation in the search for his own language."[7] By providing him with a non-metaphysical register for thinking and writing, Heidegger experienced a kind of "loosening of his tongue that occurred in his interpretation of Hölderlin's poetry."

Yet what also emerges in Heidegger's encounter with Hölderlin is a deep and abiding concern for the question of poetic dwelling. Heidegger now rethinks Hölderlin's poetic verse about such dwelling from "In lovely blueness . . ." to take up questions of how to comport ourselves, how to live, how to dwell, questions that came to concern him in his 1927 treatise *Being and Time.* Now Heidegger will rethink the centrality of Dasein within his thinking and begin to address such questions in terms of the human sojourn or *Aufenthalt* upon the earth. Two of the most thoughtful philosophers to take up the issue of an "ethics" in Heidegger remind us to be wary of any easy solution. Dennis Schmidt argues: "I am sure that Heidegger would find the very idea of developing an ethical sense out of his work

---

[6] This phrase – "den Führer führen" comes from a remark of Karl Jaspers on Heidegger's ambitions for his rectorship. Cf. Otto Pöggeler, "Den Führer führen? Heidegger und kein Ende," *Philosophische Rundschau* 32 (1985): 26–67.
[7] Hans-Georg Gadamer, *Gesammelte Werke,* III (Tübingen: Mohr-Siebeck, 1992), 327–328, 317.

problematic – at best. I suspect as well that he would have argued that all talk of ethics is premature – at best."[8] Nonetheless, Schmidt claims, we can find in "Heidegger's call for ethics to become more 'original' – that is, closer to the sources of life – . . . hints for understanding how one is to think the challenges of ethical life." Schmidt writes thoughtfully about the kinds of ethical impulses he finds in Heidegger's work, especially by showing us "how the task of philosophy belongs intimately to the task of finding an ethical sense." In a similar vein, the French philosopher Jean-Luc Nancy makes a strong case that "Heidegger's thinking itself [be] conceived of as a fundamental ethics."[9] As Nancy argues, what stands out in Heidegger's work is "the thinking of language and poetry as a true *ethos*." For Nancy, Heidegger's entire project that grows out of thinking *Dasein* in *Being and Time* constitutes a thinking of what Heidegger in "Letter on Humanism" names an "originary ethics" (GA 9: 356/PM: 271). In toto, Nancy makes a strong case that "only those who have read Heidegger blindly, or not at all, have been able to think of him as a stranger to ethical preoccupations."

What emerges from this careful work is a more nuanced approach to Heidegger's thinking, one that understands that in his later work Heidegger becomes preoccupied by thinking *ethos* in a poetic, non-metaphysical register. The crucial contributions of Will McNeill, Francois Raffoul, and Johanna Hodge (among others) have shown us how, in Heidegger's own work, we find "attempts to rethink the very site of ethics" and how, "in uncovering a more originary sense of ethics as 'authentic dwelling,'" we enter into the heart of Heidegger's difficult engagement with the tradition.[10] As we approach Heidegger's reading of Hölderlin, we would do well to keep in mind this ethical dimension of his work. For, as I see it, Heidegger's poetic thinking will come to us as "ethical" in a new and radical sense that breaks with the metaphysical tradition of ethics. *Ethos* here will be thought as our abode, our sojourn upon the earth.[11] This is Heidegger's radical, revolutionary insight – that "ethics," as it is currently constituted, is tied to structures that block our relation to genuine thinking and that what is needed instead is a new *ethos* that draws on the ancient Greek sense of that word. In *The Iliad* (Bk, VI, v. 511), Homer deploys the term *ethea* to refer to the places where animals belong, the haunts and pastures that

---

[8] Dennis Schmidt, "Ethics after Heidegger," in Gregory Fried & Richard Polt, eds., *After Heidegger?* (London: Rowman and Littlefield, 2018), 133–140.

[9] Jean-Luc Nancy, *A Finite Thinking* (Stanford: Stanford University Press, 2003), 173–174.

[10] François Raffoul, *The Origins of Responsibility* (Bloomington: Indiana University Press, 2010), 222; William McNeill, *The Time of Life: Heidegger and 'Ethos* (Albany: State University of New York Press, 2007), Johanna Hodge, *Heidegger and Ethics* (London: Routledge, 1995).

[11] Charles Bambach, "Sojourn," in Mark Wrathall, ed., *Heidegger Lexicon* (Cambridge: Cambridge University Press, 2020), 685–689.

they habitually frequent.[12] The very movement or conduct of the animal, the way it habitually returns to its haunts, its stable (the place where animals gather and abide), constitutes their *ethos*. Heidegger draws on this sense of *ethos* in his own work. As Dennis Schmidt puts it, "When Heidegger speaks of the 'basic meaning' of the word *ethos*, he refers to the way it means something like a native place or the place where something belongs and flourishes."[13] But Schmidt also reminds us of another dimension of a language attuned to the possibility of poetical dwelling and to what he calls "the enigma of ethical life."[14] Like Schmidt, I too find in Heidegger the sense that "words like 'ethics' and 'justice' no longer suffice as cues for what it is that the present historical juncture most needs."[15] What makes Heidegger's language so difficult to grasp and, if we might say, "non-fungible" is that it resists any attempt to "apply" its insights in any functional or serviceable way.

Poetic dwelling calls for a different kind of attuned experience of language, a strange and uncanny awareness of the enigmas of ethical life that cannot be circumscribed in rules, coda, maxims, or commandments. For such a language of enigma, Heidegger turns to the poetry of Hölderlin, nurtured on the tragic language of Sophocles, who tutored him in the paradoxes of *das Rätsel* (Gk, *ainigma*). Thus, in reflecting on the plight of Oedipus – that "the riddle (*das Rätsel*) was not for every man/ to solve" (OT 393) – Hölderlin would recognize that the riddle of knowledge is how "it provokes itself to know more than it can bear or grasp."[16] The enigma does not open itself to the language of conceptuality, but comes to us as an aporia. In the "Afterword" to his famous essay "The Origin of the Work of Art," Heidegger writes that his essay "concerns the enigma (*Rätsel*) of art, the enigma that art itself is. Such a claim remains far removed from solving the enigma. What stands as the task is to see the enigma" (GA 5: 67). *Ethos*, if it is anything, remains the most enigmatic sphere of human dwelling and can never be "solved" to conform to the reigning concerns of our historical life. For Heidegger, questions of ethics are more properly understood as reflections on the meaning of a Hölderlin poem or a Sophoclean tragedy and not as a treatise on human morality. Ethics begins in uncertainty and aporia where the rule does not fit the case and where calculation cannot fit the

---

[12] For a fuller discussion, cf. Charles Bambach, "The Ethos of Dwelling in *Heidegger's Letter on Humanism*" *International Yearbook for Hermeneutics* 15 (2016): 90–107, esp. 98–99.

[13] Dennis Schmidt, "On the Sources of Ethical Life," *Research in Phenomenology* 42 (2012): 35–48, here 37.

[14] Dennis Schmidt, "Ethics after Heidegger," 136.

[15] Dennis Schmidt, *On Germans and Other Greeks: Tragedy and Ethical Life* (Bloomington: Indiana University Press, 2000), 261.

[16] Friedrich Hölderlin, DKV II:803, 852/*Essays and Letters*, eds. Jeremy Adler & Charlie Louth (Hammondsworth: Penguin, 2009), 320.

circumstance. And it is precisely this incalculability that haunts ethics and that marks our abode, sojourn or *Aufenthalt* – that is, our *ethos* – as what is strange, alien, improper, even uncanny. At the very site of our dwelling, where we believe ourselves to be at home, there perdures a strange otherness that turns us away from our habits and habitudes toward the site of the inhabitual and monstrous. It is precisely this monstrousness that continues to haunt us in our haunts, threatening to dislodge us from our lodgings. In the terms we have been employing here, at the very heart of our abode, our *ethos*, lies a haunting sense that we are not at home in our haunts. Heidegger found this sense of the unhomely expressed most powerfully in poetic language – as in Trakl's verse from "Springtime of the Soul":

> The soul is a stranger on the earth.[17]

As he reads Heidegger's own notion of an "originary ethics," Jean-Luc Nancy conceives this to be nothing less than "an ethics of haunting":

> To think is neither to predict nor to prophesy nor to deliver messages,
> but to expose oneself to what happens with time, in time. In the
> time of haunting there can and must be a thinking and an ethics
> – if ethics it is – of haunting.[18]

For Nancy, ethics involves an exposure to that which haunts us, a becoming at home with what radically threatens our home, an opening or exposing ourselves to the enigma of ethical life. In his WS 1934/35 lectures on Hölderlin, Heidegger thoughtfully takes up the issue of exposure and approaches it as what holds open a relation to our historical situation and to the very sense of what poetry means.

2.2 Hölderlin Lectures on *Germania*

In these crucial lectures, Heidegger signals a clear interest in the poetic work of Hölderlin – but beyond that of the essential role that *Dichtung* plays in his thinking (not merely "poetry" as a genre of verse-making or poesy but, rather, as a "poetic composing" or "poetizing"). Here he thinks "poetizing as the fundamental event of the historical Dasein of human beings" (GA 39: 76/HGR: 68). Drawing on the German sense of *Dichten* as poetic composing (with roots in the Latin verb *dicere* – "to say or tell" [*sagen*]), Heidegger goes farther back to the sense of "poetic" from the Greek *poiesis*, which means "making" or "producing" (GA 39: 24/HGR: 29). Nonetheless, he claims that if we follow such a path set forth by etymology, "we will not attain any knowledge of the essence of what is

[17] Georg Trakl, "Frühling der Seele," *Die Dichtungen* (Salzburg: Otto Müller, 1938), 147.
[18] Jean-Luc Nancy, *A Finite Thinking*, 136.

dichterisch or poetic." "Poetizing," Heidegger tells us, "is a telling in the manner of a making manifest that points." Here again Heidegger will turn to Hölderlin's poem "In lovely blueness" with its verses on "poetic dwelling" and emphasize that "the poetic" is not a cultural manifestation or a literary enterprise. On the contrary, poetry is nothing less than "an exposure to beyng (*Ausgesetztheit dem Seyn*), and as such exposure is the fundamental occurrence of the historical Dasein of the human being" (GA 39: 36/HGR: 34). Moreover, Hölderlin's image of the poetic dwelling of the human being upon the earth does not constitute either an anthropological or historical claim in itself. As Heidegger well understands, "Human beings or a people (*Volk*) can certainly be exiled from this poetic dwelling." What Hölderlin's poetizing makes manifest, rather, is how endangered our poetic dwelling truly is and that we can only come into the promise of such dwelling if we "approach that domain in which Hölderlin's poetry unfolds its power and indeed expose ourselves to it" (GA 39: 8/HGR: 7).

As this "exposure to beyng," the poetic "tears us away" (*reisst uns*) in a turbulence that unsettles us and that "determines in turn the exposure of Dasein that has occurred in the midst of beings" (GA 39: 45, 223/HGR: 44, 203). There are several things to notice here in Heidegger's discourse about "exposure" and "tearing." In both GA 39 and in his 1936 Rome lecture, "Hölderlin and the Essence of Poetry," Heidegger cites a fragment from the famous Hellingrath edition of Hölderlin's work about "language, that most dangerous of goods" being given to the human being so that it "might bear witness to what it is . . ." (GA 4: 35/EHP: 54 tm; GA 39: 60–62/HGR: 56–58). Language is dangerous, Heidegger tells us, because it exposes us to beyng and its manifestations. Much as Semele was exposed to the overwhelming power of Zeus, resulting in her destruction, so too the poet risks being consumed by the fiery power of language as what can overcome and consume him. In his festal hymn "As on a Holiday . . .," Hölderlin places poets into an intimate relation with Semele, seeing both as figures exposed to the power and force of divine manifestation in the lightning and thunder of the sky god. As Hölderlin puts it, much as Semele was "divinely struck" (v. 52) by Zeus and therewith "gave birth to/ the thunder – storm's fruit, to holy Bacchus," so too now poets, in their own now divinely charged moment, "drink heavenly fire" (DKV I: 240).[19] And yet, despite such danger – or, rather, owing to it – Hölderlin attests:

> . . . it is fitting for us poets
> to stand beneath the god's thunderstorms with heads bared . . . (vv. 56–57)
> for only though such exposure may poetic song be birthed.

---

[19] This stems from Friedrich Hölderlin's hymn, "Wie wenn am Feiertage . . .," DKV I: 239–241/ *Selected Poems and Fragments* (London: Penguin, 2000), 172–177.

As Heidegger sees it, the thinker's task is to hear this poetic word and to enter into conversation (*Gespräch*) with it. Again, citing Hölderlin's draft "*Versöhnender der du nimmergeglaubt . . .*,"

> Much has the human being experienced.
> Has named many of the Heavenly Ones,
> Since we have been a conversation
> And can hear from one another.

Heidegger constates that "human being is grounded in conversation" (GA 4: 38, 40).[20] Moreover, he affirms that "language is the supreme event of human existence" and that "poetry is the founding of being in words" (GA 4: 40–42). Heidegger focuses here upon the poetic image of what Hölderlin names *die reissende Zeit* ("the time that tears") from the elegy "The Archipelagus" (v. 293) and from a draft for the hymn "The Titans" (v. 67). It is this phenomenon of tearing that will come to preoccupy us as we turn our attention to Heidegger's reading of Hölderlin, especially his lectures on "The Ister" that deal with the power of rivers as they tear apart the land and leave the scissions of their forceful movement upon the landscape. Yet it is the "rupture that is wrought by the tearing of time" – "its being torn open into presence, past and future" – that shapes our relation to being, as what comes to language in Greek tragic understanding.[21] It is the power of this poetic word – uttered in Greek tragedy and taken up again by Hölderlin in his festal singing of the Greek bequest – that leads Heidegger to see poetizing as the authentic founding of being in the word. What this signifies for human beings can hardly be overestimated.

"In conversation (*Gespräch*)," Heidegger tells us, "language occurs and this occurrence is properly its beyng. We are – an event of language (*ein Sprachgeschehnis*) . . ." (GA 39: 69–70/HGR: 63–64). Indeed, "our beyng occurs as conversation." This happens fundamentally in different temporal configurations that shape the historical Dasein of the human being. Yet during all of their different historical manifestations, what stands out for Heidegger is the distinctive way that language as conversation happens in its most originary sense as poetizing. Here poetizing is to be understood not as one possible form of linguistic expression among others, but as that which enables human dwelling upon the earth. "Poetizing

---

[20] This fragment occurs in different versions of Friedrich Hölderlin's hymn "Friedensfeier." Cf. Michael Knaupp's edition of Hölderlin, *Sämtliche Werke und Briefe, I* (Darmstadt: Wissenschaftliche Buchgesellschaft, 1998), 361 and 364.

[21] For an excellent account of *reissen* and *Riss* in Hölderlin, cf. William McNeill, "Remains: Heidegger and Hölderlin Amid the Ruins of Time," in Charles Bambach & Theodore George, eds., *Philosophers and Their Poets* (Albany: SUNY Press, 2019), 159–184, esp.160–163.

configures the ground of historical Dasein," Heidegger announces. It is language that *exposes* human beings to beings in such a way that it brings being to language in and as conversation. But here Heidegger stresses that such conversation is not to be understood as that which enables "communication" (*Mitteilung*) or the exchange of tidings and information. *Gespräch* first enables history to be at all. "This conversation that is a beginning, however, is poetizing and 'poetically dwells/the human being upon this earth.' Its Da-sein, as historical, has its steadfast ground in the conversation of poetizing" (GA 39: 67–70/HGR: 62–64). Moreover, in this context of emphasizing the centrality of "conversation" to his reading of poetry – and to Hölderlin – Heidegger thinks language in a decisive and revolutionary way from out of his approach to poetizing. In the Germania lectures, he will express his funda-mental understanding of language in a way that prefigures his emphasis on language in his work of the 1950s. As he formulates it, "Language is the most dangerous of goods for the human being for it exposes humans to the realm of being . . ." (GA 39: 74/HGR: 67). Heidegger goes on to emphasize that: "Language is therefore not something that the human being has, but the reverse: that which has the human being. What the human being is – we are a conversation. We are since we have been a conversation, claimed by, and brought to, language."[22]

As Heidegger comes to rethink the relationship of language to the human being and of the human being to language, he inevitably turns to Hölderlin. Within such a configuration, Heidegger will emphasize the political dimension of the poetic word as that which can properly found the historical Dasein of the German Volk. Yet Heidegger conceives his task here as less a literary analysis of Hölderlin's poetry, than as a challenge to the German people to become authentically the Volk that it is capable of becoming. In this sense, Heidegger's lectures on Hölderlin's hymn "Germania" do not offer anything like an application of the text as much as they pose a question to their audience: "Who are we?" (GA 39: 48–49). And how might "we" (the authentic German Volk) come to know ourselves? Heidegger will affirm that the historical Dasein of a Volk "springs from poetry" – but not in the sense that a Volk must read poetic verses to find its authentic identity. What is required, rather, is "a new mandate" (*Auftrag*) that might "assure the historical mission (*Sendung*) of a Volk" (GA 39: 99/HGR: 90). But in an age where the gods have fled and faith in historical regeneration has flagged from out of the exhaus-tion of the Great War and the cultural pessimism of decline (Spengler) that attends its demise, Heidegger seizes on the political hope of a coming transformation

---

[22] In two essays from 1951 "Building Dwelling Thinking" and ". . . poetically dwells the human being," Heidegger offers an account of the relation between human beings and language in terms that echo his insights from GA 39: "The human being behaves as if *he* were the sculptor and master of language, whereas it is *language* that remains the sovereign of the human being" GA 7: 148, 193/PLT: 146, 215 tm). Cf. also GA 16:331.

whose promise he locates in Hölderlin. In these same lectures Heidegger affirms that *"The 'fatherland' is beyng itself"* (GA 39: 121/HGR: 109). Yet what the fatherland "is" and who we "are" remains "sealed in a mystery (*Geheimnis*) and indeed essentially and forever." It is this trope of a secret, mysterious bond to the fatherland, expressed publicly for the first time in the Hölderlin lectures that will come to shape key elements in Heidegger's relation to the poet and to poetic thinking. For what will mark this lecture course and the two that follow in WS 1941/42, *Hölderlin's Hymn 'Remembrance'* and in SS 1942, *Hölderlin's Hymn 'The Ister,'* is a powerful commitment to Hölderlin as the poet of a "secret Germany," not the public "Germany" that goes under the name of the thousand-year Reich.

In the early years of Hitler's reign, Heidegger will publicly support the National Socialist party and aspire to become an influence in NS educational policy through his role as rector of Freiburg University. Once he realizes that the NS power structure has no place for him within its machinational ambitions, he abandons his public role as rector and adopts a more nuanced stance toward Germany's political future. Against this background, in his Black Notebooks, Heidegger puts forward what he terms a "metapolitics," one that will bring about: *"The end of "philosophy"* – We must bring it to an end and thereby what is wholly other – metapolitics" (GA 94: 115/BN I: 85).

Here Heidegger self-consciously announces that "the *metaphysics* of Dasein" that he put forward in *Being and Time* "must become deeper in accord with the innermost structure of that metaphysics and must expand into a metapolitics 'of' the historical Volk" (GA 94: 124/BN I: 91). The editor of the Black Notebooks, Peter Trawny, has argued that Hölderlin "has a crucial role at the very center of [Heidegger's] 'metapolitics of the historical Volk.'"[23] As he forges his own style of poetic thinking, Heidegger undertakes a radical rethinking of the political that endows the Germans with the revolu-tionary task of "saving the West" (GA 80: 693). Beginning in WS 1934/35, we could make the case that Heidegger abandons his hopes for a public-political revolution led by Hitler and the National Socialist party. Now Heidegger will embrace the dream of a "secret Germany" promulgated in the writings of Norbert von Hellingrath. This dream positions the German Volk at the epi-center of a transition to an other beginning for thinking, one nurtured on the poetic language of Hölderlin. In his *Hölderlin-Vermächtnis*, Hellingrath deems Hölderlin as the voice of Germany's futural mission of rousing the West from its slumberous negligence of its ancient Greek legacy. Hellingrath finds in Hölderlin's translations of Pindar and Sophocles the signs of a special,

---

[23] Peter Trawny, *Heidegger: Eine kritische Einführung* (Frankfurt: Klostermann, 2016), 87.

inner bond between the Greek and German languages that authorizes the German people to take up the mission of the Greeks. Not only in the resonance, modulation, tone, and rhythm of Pindar's verse or in Sophocles' elliptical language of reversal and ambiguity, but also in the inner structure and ligatures of Greek and German grammar and syntax, Hellingrath finds a native affinity.[24] As Hellingrath expresses it, "I name Hölderlin the most German of poets ... because he counts, justifiably, as the most Greek." Moreover, Hellingrath contends that "Hölderlin's turn to the fatherland is only the direct consequence of his Greek being." It is this "dream of Hellas" that shapes Hellingrath's vision of the German Volk as the one "especially chosen" to take up the mission of bringing the German Volk, the German nation, and the German language home to its native identity. As Hellingrath put it:

> I call us "the Volk of Hölderlin" because it is of the very essence of the Germans that their innermost, fervid core (which lies infinitely deep beneath the veneer of its dross-covered crust) can only come to light in a *secret* Germany. This innermost core expresses itself through human beings who, at the very least, must be long dead before they are recognized and find a response; and works that will always impart their secret only to the very few, saying nothing to most, and wholly inaccessible to non-Germans. Indeed, this is true because this secret Germany is so certain of its inner value ... that it makes no effort to be heard or seen ... Hölderlin is the greatest example of this hidden fire, of this secret Reich, of the still unrecognized coming into being of the divine burning core.[25]

The inspiration for this grand design of a secret Germany, inaccessible to the many, concealed in mystery and enigma, lay in Hölderlin's fragment "Einst hab' ich die Muse gefragt" ("Once I asked the Muse"), a crucial text that Heidegger cites on several occasions.

> Of that which is Highest, I wish to be silent.
> Forbidden fruit, like the laurel, is, however,
> Above all, the fatherland. Such, however,
> Each will taste last of all. (GA 39: 4, 220; GA 52: 134; GA 16: 334)

Yet, Hölderlin warns us,
> In the end, no mortal can grasp it. (DKV I: 393)

For Hellingrath, this hidden dimension of the fatherland comprises what is most worthy of seeking within it. For what is present before us in the historical moment does not reflect the essence of the fatherland. Germania

---

[24] Norbert von Hellingrath, *Hölderlin-Vermächtnis* (Munich: Bruckmann, 1944), 104, 125.

[25] Norbert von Hellingrath, *Hölderlin-Vermächtnis*, 120–121.

stands forth as "the chosen one" (*Auserwählte*) – and, most of all – owing to its "language."[26] For Hellingrath, it is only "in poetic words that are not revealed to the uninitiated" that the promise of the fatherland may be spoken. Hellingrath delivered these remarks in a 1915 speech "Hölderlin and the Germans" as Germany was in the midst of fighting a world war that was to claim Hellingrath's life at Verdun in December 1916. When, a generation later, Heidegger takes up these same themes in his first Hölderlin lecture course, there reigns the hope of German national renewal out of the ashes of the Great War. In a lecture held in the summer of 1934, "The Contemporary Situation and the Future Task of German Philosophy," Heidegger speaks of a new "mandate and mission" for German thinking, one that needs to attune itself to the poetic language of Hölderlin (GA 16: 332–333). If "the lightning flashes of the gods strike us and the world-hour of the Volk comes to word," then Germany can "go forward to meet a new day of its history." Such a transformation "does not require the pre-arranged pseudo-community of a 'League of Nations'"; its possibility depends, rather, on creating a community of those who might hear the poet's words and realize a new *kerygma*, one announced by Heidegger at the end of his first Hölderlin course.

> The hour of our history has struck. We must first take what has been given us as endowment (*das Mitgegebene*) into pure safekeeping once again, yet only so as to comprehend and take hold of what has been given as our task (*das Aufgegebene*) – that is, to question our way forward and through it. The violence of beyng must first and actually become a question again for our ability to grasp (*Fassenkönnen*). (GA 39: 294/HGR: 266)

These are Heidegger's final words of the course from WS 1934/35 and they echo in striking ways the final paragraph of the course Heidegger delivered on *Logic as the Question Concerning the Essence of Language* from the previous semester SS1934. There, in a course that reverses the priority of logic to language, Heidegger finds in poetry the originary essence of language ("Originary language is the language of poetizing," GA 38: 170). And though Heidegger does not explicitly name Hölderlin here, he does adopt the same strategy as in the Germania/Rhine lecture course. That is, he concludes by returning to the question of German identity that is bound up with the question of what is native to the Germans as *endowment* and what has been given to them as their *task*. In the Logic course he admonishes the Germans that if they wish to grasp their own poetic language, they "must learn what it means to preserve

---

[26] Norbert von Hellingrath, *Hölderlin-Vermächtnis*, 146–147.

(*bewahren*) what they already possess (*besitzen*)."[27] Two points are worthy of our attention here. As Heidegger comes to think of the authentic task "of" the Germans, he takes up Hellingrath's theme that their "elected" status lies in the gift of language – "the flower of the mouth" ("Germania," v. 72) – granted them by the eagle of Zeus, come to awaken the Volk from its slumbers. Here we find the outlines of Hellingrath's reading of Hölderlin's "dream of Hellas" that it is time for the poet to recognize Germania as "the chosen one," but also to acknowledge that the task set before the German Volk by Zeus' emissary requires that they "bear a grave good fortune" ("ein schweres Glück . . . tragen," "Germania," vv. 63–64).

The task of becoming German will be difficult. To possess that which is native to one requires a journey, an encounter, what Hölderlin will term "ein Ausflug" into what is foreign. In undergoing this struggle to become who they are, the Germans come to embrace the rhythm of all being that "consists in the alternation of opening and closing, in departure and return to itself" (*in Ausflug und in Rückkehr zu sich selbst*).[28] In this model of departure and return, identity emerges out of an authentic encounter with difference whereby what is native to one's own (*das Eigene*) can only be approached via a journey to the foreign (*das Fremde*). This profound insight into what Heidegger would later call "the law of history" finds its paradigmatic expression in a letter that Hölderlin wrote to his friend Casimir Ulrich Böhlendorff on December 4, 1801 on the eve of his life-altering journey to Bordeaux.[29] In this letter, Hölderlin offers his own account of the relation between ancient Greek and modern German art – specifically, the attempt by nineteenth-century German poets to write "tragedy." As Hölderlin counsels his friend:

> Nothing is harder for us to learn than to freely use the national . . . But the ownmost (*das Eigene*) must be learned as well as the foreign (*das Fremde*). That is why the Greeks are indispensable to us. Only it is precisely in what is

---

[27] Two things should be noticed here – firstly, that in employing the word "bewahren" Heidegger is drawing our attention to the poetic relation to truth (*Wahrheit*). Secondly, there is an allusion to Johann Wolfgang von Goethe's, *Faust* I that plays upon one of the most familiar lines of German literature: "Was du erebt von deinen Vätern hast/ Erwirb es, um es zu besitzen!" cited from the dual language edition of Walter Kaufmann, *Goethe's Faust* (New York: Doubleday, 1961), 114–115.

[28] Friedrich Hölderlin, DKV II: 46.

[29] Friedrich Hölderlin, DKV III: 459–462. In this famous letter to Böhlendorff, Hölderlin outlines a philosophy of history that shows the determinative role played by Greek art. There he distinguishes between the Greeks and what he terms the "Hesperians" (i.e., modern Germans). The term *Hesperian* is taken from the Roman poet Lucan's text *Pharsalia (The Civil War)* (Cambridge: Harvard University Press, 1988), 30–32. Hölderlin translated the first book of *Pharsalia* into German, DKV II: 638–661, esp., 653–654. Hesperia refers to the modern Western world of Europe north of the Alps in contrast to the ancient lands of sub-Alpine Greece and Rome. For Hölderlin, this becomes linked to both "das Vaterländische" and "das Deutsche," DKV III:467.

proper to us, in the national, that we shall never match them since, as said, the free use of what is one's own is most difficult.[30]

For Heidegger, this single letter written to Böhlendorff will come to play an inordinate role, not only in how he comes to think of Hölderlin's poetic legacy, but also in terms of how he will come to understand the enigma of poetic dwelling. Heidegger will underscore the significance of this letter – the one Hellingrath designates as "the most important letter" of Hölderlin's since it serves as "the source for Hölderlin's thinking" – in every one of his Hölderlin courses, in his book *Elucidations of Hölderlin's Poetry* and in "The Western Conversation" (GA 4: 82, 157–159, 175; GA 39: 31, 136, 211, 242, 290–293; GA 52: 180–193; GA 53: 154–160; 168–169; 175–180; and GA 75: 345–347, 357).[31] What the Böhlendorff letter comes to signify for Heidegger is a radically new form of poetic dwelling, one whereby the German Volk embrace their bond to the ancient Greeks in a reversal that acknowledges the supreme importance of the foreign, the strange, the uncanny. The logic of such a claim lies in the curious and intimate relation of the Greek-Hesperian axis. For Heidegger, poetic dwelling involves the task of appropriating what is properly one's own. But as the Böhlendorff letter stresses, this is what is precisely "most difficult." Because what is one's own, *das Eigene*, lies all too near to us, properly dwelling in such nearness (*Nähe*) proves to be the most difficult since its very proximity inures us to what is authentically our own within it. The difficulty is poetized in Hölderlin's magisterial hymn "Patmos," whose opening verses announce:

> Near is
> And difficult to grasp, the God. (DKV I: 350)

So too for Heidegger, it is the very nearness of German destiny that requires a sojourn (*Aufenthalt*) into the foreign.

As he put it in his famous *Der Spiegel* interview of 1966, it is this "special inner kinship of the German language with the language of the Greeks and their thinking" that continued to exert its influence until the very end of Heidegger's life. Heidegger's enduring question, which came to shape the very contours of his poetic thinking, would be expressed as a question about our proper way of dwelling. In a late speech from 1969 in Amriswil, Heidegger cites the opening

---

[30] Friedrich Hölderlin, DKV III: 459–460/E&L: 207–208. Cf. also the translation by Dennis Schmidt in *On Germans and Other Greeks*, 135–147 and 165–167. For another analysis, see Charles Bambach, *Of an Alien Homecoming*, (Albany: SUNY Press, 2022), 84–88 and 177–184.

[31] Friedrch Hölderlin, *Sämtliche Werke*, V, ed. Norbert von Hellingrath (Munich: Propyläen, 1923), 373. In GA 75, "Das Abendländische Gespräch," Heidegger does not explicitly refer to the Böhlendorff letter, but the dialogue is nonetheless shaped by its themes.

verse from a late poem of Hölderlin's in Hellingrath's edition, "Der Herbst" ("Autumn") – "The gleaming of nature is higher revelation" (DKV I: 470). And then Heidegger proceeds:

> And when we ask about the sojourn of modern humanity in the present word epoch, we ask: Is there still a gleaming of nature? Is there still a revelation? Is there still even a higher revelation . . .?
>
> The gleaming nature is distorted (*verstellt*) . . . in the figure that human machination produces (*herstellt*) and requisitions for itself (*sich bestellt*) . . . .
>
> So it comes to be that contemporary humanity can not see, let alone question, where it resides (*sich aufhält*) . . . . (GA 16: 716–717)

As Heidegger puts it: "Modern technology and with it the scientific industrialization of the world set themselves about through their incessant planning to extinguish every possibility of sojourning (*Aufenthalten*)" (GA 75: 244). This lifelong preoccupation with the sojourn, abode, *ethos*, and *Aufenthalt* of the human being is unthinkable in Heidegger's sense without his lifelong conversation with Hölderlin. If the task of poetic thinking can be understood as finding our poetic dwelling upon the earth, then it is essential that we "experience the beyng-historical position of Hölderlin in the singularity of his anticipatory poetic vocation, one that poetically grounds the other beginning of our history" (GA 75: 336). For direction in helping the Germans find their home, Heidegger turns to those figures from Greek antiquity who come to manifest the homelessness of the human being in an uncanny sense. In Hölderlin's poetic encounter with Sophoclean tragedy – especially the figure of Oedipus and his daughter/sister Antigone – Heidegger comes to find a way of restaging the encounter between the native and the foreign that powerfully enunciates a way of dwelling as a "becoming homely" in "being unhomely": "such dwelling, however, being properly homely, is 'poetic'" (GA 53: 171/ HI: 137). It is this encounter with Greek tragedy that becomes essential to Heidegger's poetic thinking between 1935 and 1942.

3 Sophocles' *Antigone*: An Ethics of the Uncanny

3.1 The Shift in Heidegger's Thinking of Greek Tragedy (1935–1942)

In a short Element such as this, we cannot do justice to the many shifts, detours, turnings, and transitions on Heidegger's formidable *Denkweg*. But here we need to stop and reflect on a crucial turn within Heidegger's thinking from an emphasis on *Kampf*, struggle, *polemos*, violence, and martial opposition in the early 1930s to one that embraces what Bret Davis emphasizes as a new opening to letting-be, releasement, and a middle-voiced inflection of nonwilling – away from

Heidegger's earlier emphasis on *Kampf -Gewalt* -Self-Assertion – and a politics of the will.[32] Davis identifies a problematic strain of violence in Heidegger's 1935 lecture course *Introduction to Metaphysics*. We see this, Davis argues, in Heidegger's "deployment of military metaphor [where] the relation between man and being is thought in terms of power and violence, that is, as 'the *polemos* of *physis* and the violent essence of the human being'." Claire Geiman has also written on Heidegger's 1935 lecture course in a deeply engaging way but, unlike Davis, she focuses her attention on Heidegger's interpretation of Sophocles' tragedy *Antigone*, especially its first stasimon.[33] On Geiman's reading, we need to take notice of the dramatic shift in Heidegger's two separate interpretations from the 1935 course and from the SS 1942 course on *Hölderlin's Hymn 'The Ister.'* Geiman underscores how, in the first course, Heidegger approaches the play in terms of an understanding of human knowing as *techne*. Here, Geiman argues, Heidegger defines *techne* as "violent disclosure in world-creation." In the intervening years between the two courses, she notices "a move away from the violence of knowing" and an opening to a new kind of poetic thinking anchored in an interpretation of Hölderlin. Now, in SS 1942, force and compulsion (two determinative themes in GA 40) are viewed as what occludes any possibility of dwelling poetically. What unquestionably differentiates these two separate readings of Antigone is that only in the second one do we explicitly find the formidable voice of Hölderlin.

In this section, we will look at the decisive shift in Heidegger's turn toward poetic thinking as we examine his engagement with Greek tragedy, specifically the reading he performs of Sophocles' play *Antigone*. Heidegger situates such a reading in the middle of his thinking about the earliest thinkers of the Greek tradition – Anaximander, Heraclitus, and Parmenides. In *Introduction to Metaphysics*, Heidegger will set poetizing and thinking into a new order of rank above the traditional sciences and above philosophy. There he will argue that "in comparison to all mere science (*Wissenschaft*), an essential superiority holds sway in poetizing" (GA 40: 29/IM: 29). Moreover, Heidegger will emphasize how "the thinking of Parmenides and Heraclitus is still poetic" and how "in this poetizing-thinking, thinking has precedence" (GA 40: 153/IM: 161). Yet, Heidegger explains, in order to more properly address the power of this poetic thinking, he will need to "interrogate a thinking poetry of the Greeks.

---

[32] See Bret Davis', important book, *Heidegger and the Will: On the Way to "Gelassenheit"* (Evanston: Northwestern University Press, 2007) and the edition of *Gelassenheit* edited by Alfred Denker & Holger Zaborowski (Freiburg: Alber, 2014).

[33] Claire Geiman, "Heidegger's Antigones," in Richard Polt & Gregory Fried, eds., *A Companion to Heidegger's "Introduction to Metaphysics"* (New Haven: Yale University Press, 2001), 161–182.

This poetry is tragedy – the poetry in which Greek being and the Dasein proper to it were authentically founded." As he "recalls the originary essential connection between poetic and thoughtful saying," he will read it as that which concerns "the inceptual poetizing-thinking that grounds and founds the historical Dasein of a Volk" (GA 40: 174–176/IM 184–186). What connects thinking and poetizing is that they are both bound up "in the happening of uncanniness" (*das Geschehnis der Unheimlichkeit*). But in these 1935 lectures, Heidegger stresses how "the belonging-together of apprehending (*noein*) and being (*einai*), which is said in Parmenides" finds its correlation in Sophocles' understanding of the human being as *deinos* – the uncanniest of all creatures that journey upon the earth. We will pursue a closer reading of *deinos* as the essential word of Greek tragedy pace Heidegger, but here let us note two crucial themes in the way Heidegger develops his reading of the relation between poetizing and thinking. First of all, Heidegger lays stress on "the violence-doing" (*Gewalttätigkeit*) of the human being and chooses Oedipus as his exemplar: "Here, the uncanniest possibility of Dasein shows itself: to break the excessive violence of being through Dasein's ultimate act of violence against itself . . . for, as Dasein, it must indeed shatter against being in every act of violence" (GA 40: 186/IM: 197). It is from out of this violence, through a politics of will and self-assertion, that Heidegger hopes to fashion a new political order. It is from out of the uncanny violence of the human being – in the sense of that which expels Dasein from out of its home, from everything which is of the home or *heimisch* – that Heidegger finds the key to unlocking the understanding of Greek tragedy. In this sense, what is uncanny or *un-heimlich* is how the human being is driven out of its home by the violence of its own uncanniness that propels it forth beyond the limits of the homely. For Heidegger, it is this "saying" that "the human being is the uncanniest that provides the authentic *Greek* definition of the human being," a definition that finds its poetic expression in the first stasimon of Sophocles' *Antigone* (GA 40: 160).

The second feature of this excursus on uncanniness is how Heidegger ties the violence of Greek Dasein to his emphasis on poetic thinking. As in his Germania course from a semester earlier, Heidegger seizes upon the Heraclitean trope of *polemos* (conflict, war, battle, *Kampf*, contention) as essential to understanding that "strife (*Streit*) and battle (*Kampf*) determine everything fundamentally" (GA 39: 125). Still, here he thinks that poetic thinking offers us privileged insight into such strife since it opens a path to a fundamental attunement – what Heidegger, drawing upon Hölderlin, names "Innigkeit." Although the word *Innigkeit* may be translated as "intimacy," it does not refer to "the mere 'interiority' of sensation" (GA 39: 117/HGR: 106). Rather, "It means first, the supreme force of Dasein. Second, this force preserves itself in the most extreme conflict of beyng from the ground up. In short: *Innigkeit* (intimacy) is an attuned, knowing standing within (*Innestehen*) and carrying-out (*Austragen*) of the essential conflicts of that which, in its oppositional contrast, possesses an originary unity." In his essay "The Ground of Empedocles," Hölderlin terms such contrastive unity "the harmoniously opposed" (GA 39: 117/HGR: 106; DKV II: 428).

For Heidegger, *Innigkeit* comes to serve as the name of that "originary unity of the enmity of powers of what has purely sprung forth" (GA 39: 250/HGR: 226). Heidegger names *Innigkeit* "the foundational metaphysical word," "one of the key words for Hölderlin" (GA 39: 249, 117). On that basis alone, it would surely draw our attention. But Heidegger goes beyond this Hölderlin-focused reading to understand *Innigkeit* as the name for the intimate relation between poetizing and thinking (GA 71: 330). In "The Event," Heidegger puts it this way:

> The thinking of beyng is poetizing.
> The poetizing of the holy is a thinking. (GA 71: 328)

Heidegger then goes on to show how the relation between thinking and poetizing "resides in the intimacy (*Innigkeit*) of the most extreme discord," one whereby their very unity is woven in and through their dissension (GA 71: 330). In this Heraclitean unity of extreme conflict, Heidegger finds a pathway into Hölderlin's own sense of the unity/discord between poetry and philosophy. And perhaps here we can find at least some help in understanding why Heidegger avoids analysis of Hölderlin's essays on poetic composition and philosophy since for him they remain caught in the metaphysics of the tradition. To put it plainly: For Heidegger, Hölderlin's *Denken* remains caught in metaphysics; his poetizing, on the other hand, offers a pathway out of such metaphysics. It is in the poetry that we find a draft that Heidegger will cite on several occasions:

> Alles ist innig.
> (Everything is intimate.) (DKV I: 430; GA 4: 73, 196; GA 52: 98; GA 75: 363)

Here Hölderlin names that Heraclitean principle of *polemos* where forces of confluence come together not through agreement or compliance but through their own essential contention. As Hölderlin expressed it at the end of his novel *Hyperion*:

> The dissonances of the world are like lovers' quarrels. Reconciliation happens in the midst of strife and everything sundered finds itself again.
> (DKV II: 175)

For Heidegger, this sense of *Innigkeit* might be better understood as a being intimate *in* and *to* the strife that serves as a principle of unity. Perhaps *Innigkeit* could be translated as "conflictual intimacy," a being intimate to conflict, dissonance, strife, opposition, and alterity, a strange kind of intimacy that Heidegger sees as essential to our own possibility of poetic dwelling. What comes forth out of his engagement with the earliest Greek thinkers in the 1930s is a sense of how it might help us to experience a form of poetic thinking attuned to the other, the strange, the alien, the non-native as what enables us to dwell in the home. The outlines for such a way of thinking are articulated in *The Event* where Heidegger places poetizing and thinking in an intimate relation with the other:

Poetizing is the co-sharing of the	Thinking is the departure into the un-homely
homely in the imagistic word of the nearness of the holy.	in the imageless word of the jointure of beyng.
. . . Poetizing is becoming homely	Thinking is becoming homely
from out of being unhomely.	in being unhomely. (GA 71: 330/E: 286 tm)

It is this "law" of becoming homely from out of being unhomely – and the thinking thereof – that will come to shape one of Heidegger's most important texts, the SS 1942 lectures, *Hölderlin's Hymn 'The Ister.'*

3.2 Hölderlin and Sophocles: The Dialogue with Thinking

Heidegger is quick to remind his readers that "the thinking of the history of beyng . . . must enter into dialogue with the poetizing that poetizes the domain of poetry and thus must think through the relation between poetizing and thinking" (GA 71: 259/E: 216). As the entryway into such a relation, Heidegger chooses the dialogue between ancient Greek and modern German poetizing in the figures of Sophocles and Hölderlin. There is much to consider here. First of all, not only does the dialogue concern the intimate relation between antiquity and modernity, Greek and German, Sophocles and Hölderlin, but beyond this it concerns the relation of all these relations to a poetic thinking that sets its task as the preparation for an other beginning of thinking. Pursuing such a task, we will need to think the pivotal role played by translation and how all translation manifests the unity/difference between the native and the foreign. Within such a process, translation – understood literally as an *Über-setzung* – both places and displaces us across from and over against our native idiom. Translation shatters against the habitual practices of ordinary communication where "language" is understood as a mere exchange of information. Heidegger insists that the practice of translation exceeds the technical limits of language equivalency and concerns, rather, "the relation of the human being to the essence of the word and to the worthiness of language" (GA 53: 76/HI: 63). As the highest expression of the problem of translation, Heidegger chooses a word from Sophocles' *Antigone* that he designates as "the fundamental word of this tragedy, indeed of Greek tragedy altogether, and thereby the fundamental word of Greek antiquity" (GA 53: 82/HI: 57). This word, whose essence pervades the whole movement and trajectory of the play, is the Greek word *deinos*. Even in antiquity, the word *deinos* became the bearer of polychrome meanings simultaneously. In her recent translation of *Antigone*, Anne Carson translates it in multiple ways – as "strange," "terrible," "wondrous," "monstrous," "marvelous," "dreadful," "awful," and "weird."[34] In his initial translation of the first stasimon from *Antigone* (1799), Hölderlin had translated *deinos* as "gewaltge" (sic) or violent. In his publication of 1804, however, he revised his original version and now rendered *deinos* in German as *Ungeheuer* (monstrous, frightful, atrocious, precarious).[35] As Heidegger turned to this first stasimon from *Antigone*, he came to see *deinos* as an essential word for his own kind of poetic thinking in conversation with Sophocles and Hölderlin.

We have at least three different versions of Heidegger's translation of this ode – in his SS 1935 and SS 1942 lecture courses and in a draft from his Nachlass (GA 40: 155–157; GA 53: 71–72; GA 81: 337). In the first two texts, Heidegger renders *deinos* as *das Unheimliche*; in the third rendition, he alters this slightly and translates it as *Unheimliches* (without an adjective) – "unhomely, uncanny, that being without a home." This sense of uncanniness is *vielfältig*, the translation tells us. It has, literally, "many folds" or, as we typically say in English, this uncanniness is "manifold." Several times in his collection of Hölderlin essays compiled in GA 4, Heidegger refers to Hölderlin's poetic use of the term *Einfalt*, which is usually translated as "simplicity," but which more literally means "one fold."[36] If the signature of poetic thinking is to think being in terms of the *Einfalt* of an intimate belonging together of all that is, then it must also poetize how the human being is so situated as to be riven and torn by the manifold of forces that displace it from such intimacy. In Heidegger's rendering of Sophocles' hymn, this tear itself will come to shape his interpretation of the human being as the unhomely one, the unhomeliest of all creatures that walk upon the earth. If we follow Heidegger here, we are led into

---

[34] Sophocles, *Antigone*, translated by Anne Carson (London: Oberon Books, 2015). See also the playful, but incisive riff on Sophocles in Carson's *Antigonick* (New York: New Directions, 2015).

[35] Compare David Constantine's translation in *Hölderlin's Sophocles: Oedipus and Antigone* (Northumberland: Bloodaxe Books, 2001), 81. Constantine translates *ungeheur* as "monstrous." Cf. also DKV II: 691 where Hölderlin translates the first line of Sophocles' ode as "Vieles gewaltge gibt's" and DKV II: 873 where he translates it as: "Ungeheur ist viel."

[36] Hölderlin employs the term *Einfalt* in DKV I: 307, 335, 352, 380. "Dichterberuf" v. 62; "Patmos" v. 78; Germanien" v.50; and "Deutscher Gesang" v. 26.

a confrontation with the intimate sense of translation as an enactment of the selfsame relation of native:foreign as Hölderlin unfolds in his Böhlendorff letter. Hence, it can hardly be surprising to find Heidegger addressing the question of poetic dwelling in the Ister lectures in terms of questions about native and foreign, one's own and the other, the proper and the alien – questions that have to do with the human *Aufenthalt* or sojourn upon the earth poetized by Hölderlin in his "Rhine" hymn. There the poet reflects on the plight of the human being as it confronts

> ... the limits
> Which God at birth marked out
> For its term and stay (*Aufenthalt*). (DKV I: 331)

In reflecting on Hölderlin's way of bringing our stay, our sojourn (*Aufenthalt*) to language, Heidegger faces the very enigmas, reversals, ambiguities, and inversions that come to shape our ethical relation to the world. In an important sense, it is here in his reading of Sophocles' *Antigone* that Heidegger unfolds some of the most powerful ethical insights in his entire corpus. In his singular reading of the *Antigone* ode, over Hölderlin's shoulder as it were, Heidegger uncovers the powerful sense of Greek Dasein in terms of *ethos*, ethics, and the prospect of dwelling authentically in the homeland. Moreover, it is in these same lectures, despite their sense of German exceptionalism and the bellicose assault against what he terms "Americanism" (a kind of shorthand for machination, rootlessness, and the will to cybernetic dominion over the earth) that we find a Heidegger who takes up a fundamentally ethical reflection on the meaning of dwelling, *Aufenthalt, ethos* as what belong essentially to a new kind of poetic thinking. Here, we find crucial hints, beckonings, and intimations of an ethics that, breaking with the "ethics" of right and wrong, offers penetrating insights into a fitting relation between the proper and the strange, the native and the foreign, oneself and/as the other. If the question of ethics has to do with the authentic possibility of dwelling – and if dwelling is understood as bound up with the question of our sojourn/*ethos*/*Aufenthalt* that comes to define our habitual haunts, habitat, and settlement – then the question shaping the Ister lectures can be understood as fundamentally ethical since it is this question of poetic dwelling that defines our way of "being properly homely" (*das eigentliche Heimischsein*) (HI: 137/GA 53: 171). Ultimately, I will argue for what I see as a Heideggerian "ethics of the uncanny" as the basis for my claims here. But first we need to broach Heidegger's reading of the first stasimon in *Antigone*.

What matters for Heidegger in his dialogue with both Hölderlin and Sophocles is to take up the question about the uncanniness of the human being precisely as a question about human dwelling. Here what is at stake is less our residence, domicile, settlement, or habitat than it is a question of what Heidegger in his 1946 "Letter on Humanism" will term "originary ethics" (GA 9: 356). Tragedy offers the proper space for such inquiry since it presents the irreconcilability of those existential concerns in a language poetically attuned to just such a chiastic and unresolvable set of questions. As Jean-Pierre Vernant has put it, tragedy is perpetually marked by ambiguity, contradiction, and enigma, so much so that this tension "makes tragedy into a questioning to which there can be no answers."[37] What enables Heidegger to follow the contours and reversals of this tragic grammar can be found in his reading of the Böhlendorff letter with its logic of inversion and attunement to alterity.

As we saw earlier in the Böhlendorff letter, Hölderlin lays out there the very grammar of his poetological understanding of the native and the foreign as a way to grasp the creative relation of the Germans to the Greeks. Within eighteenth-century aesthetics, Johann Winckelmann had expressed the view that the task set for German art was to imitate the ideal of classical beauty – "noble simplicity and tranquil grandeur" – expressed in sculptural form in the Apollo Belvedere. As Winckelmann put it: "The only way for us to become great and (if it is possible) inimitable, is in imitating the ancients ...."[38] Yet Hölderlin, whose love of Greek culture was certainly intense, would have none of Winckelmann's uncritical veneration of the ancients. As he saw it, the task of the Germans lay not in mimesis, but in critical appropriation and confrontation with antiquity. As Hölderlin put it in "The Standpoint from which we should consider Antiquity," the only path for Hesperian *Bildung* lay in a "reaction against the positive animation of that which is dead through a genuinely reciprocal union of the two."[39] In his rejection of Winckelmann's reverent adherence to the canons of ancient Greek aesthetics, what becomes essential for Hölderlin is that the Germans recognize the foreignness of the Greeks to the Germans' own native endowment. Only on this basis, in confrontation with this radically "other" Greece, can the Germans appropriate what is proper to them. We find this same logic in Hölderlin's Böhlendorff letter where he tells his friend that one's proper origin can only be appropriated when the proper is experienced as what is strange, foreign, and other. This same logic applies both to Hölderlin's poetic experience in his translations of Pindar and Sophocles and in Heidegger's engagement with them.[40] For Heidegger, such translation itself, beyond its

---

[37] Jean-Pierre Vernant & Pierre Vidal-Naquet, *Myth and Tragedy in Ancient Greece* (New York: Zone Books, 1990), 38.

[38] Johann Joachim Winckelmann, *Ausgewählte Schriften* (Wiesbaden: Dieterich, 1948), 3.

[39] Friedrich Hölderlin, DKV II: 508/E&L:247.

[40] For a fuller discussion of what I call Hölderlin's "Böhlendorff logic," see Charles Bambach, *Thinking the Poetic Measure of Justice*: *Hölderlin-Heidegger-Celan* (Albany: SUNY Press, 2013), 46–53.

status as an originary poetic work, becomes the model for his own poetic thinking. As he expresses it in his *Nachlass*:

> Trans-lation – to another shore – on the shore of the Other!!/
> Über-setzen – auf ein anderes Ufer – an das Ufer eines Anderen!! (GA 75: 343)

If traditional translation follows the Winckelmannian logic of imitation, correspondence, and mimesis, Hölderlin's translation strives for an aesthetic of rupture, scission, caesura, and estrangement. Such a practice sets the performative stage for Heidegger's own interpretation of Sophocles' *Antigone* in conversation with this Hölderlinian project.

3.3 An Ethics of the Uncanny: Reading Heidegger's Antigone

Before embarking on a fuller discussion of the ethical questions that lie at the center of Sophocles' *Antigone* – especially in the first stasimon – we will need to recognize how Heidegger approaches these questions within his lecture course of SS 1942. After a long discussion of rivers, poetry, and the tension between staying at home and journeying, Heidegger interrupts his lecture course on Hölderlin's hymn, "The Ister," to focus on "The Greek Interpretation of Human Beings in Sophocles' *Antigone*." For the original audience, this sharp shift of focus must have appeared strange and unorthodox. In the middle of an analysis on rivers and dwelling in the modern German homeland, we suddenly move to a consideration of antiquity and the role that tragic language plays in the composition and poetic architecture of the river hymns. And yet as we look more closely, we begin to notice some striking parallels between the poetizing of rivers and the Sophoclean topos of dwelling and/in the uncanny. At one point in the lecture course, Heidegger comes to consider the role of the poet as the one who composes the river hymn whereby he emphasizes that the poet here is no longer a singular, detached figure whose ground lies in the "subjectivity" of human beings. In exposing himself to the dangers of the discordant forces that pervade the river, the poet achieves an intimacy with it that discloses a deeper union. In just such a relation of intimacy, the discord joins into a conflictual harmony that bespeaks the mystery of authentic dwelling. Now, as Heidegger puts it, "The poet is the river. And the river is the poet" (GA 53: 203/HI: 165). At stake in such a reading is nothing less than the insight that rivers ground, poetically, the dwelling of human beings upon the earth in an originary *poiesis* that reveals the essence of the rivers as sites for such dwelling. Here rivers carry out such *poiesis* through being's own poetic power that not only allows for human dwelling but opens up such dwelling to human possibility. This profound binding of humans to rivers carries out the intimacy of their belonging together. Poetic dwelling, then, needs to be grasped as a poietic event. As William McNeill puts it in *The Time of Life*, *poiesis* first grounds our being as dwelling, appearing as "the event of an originary *poiesis* of which we are not the origin, yet which, happening in and through us, first enables our dwelling."[41] It is not the poet who establishes this relation; rather, as Heidegger attests, the river *is* the poet.

In the Ister's journey eastward to its estuary near the ancient city of Istros, a colony of Miletus, the city where Thales and Anaximander once philosophized, Hölderlin uncovers a poetic geography linking Europe to Asia, modernity to antiquity, Greeks to Germans, and philosophy to poetry. As the site of these epochal turnings and exchanges, Hölderlin imagines the path of the river undergoing a reversal.

> Yet almost this river appears
> To go backwards and
> I presume it must come
> From the East.
> Much could be said
> About this. (DKV I: 363, vv. 41–45)

As this Heraclitean river shifts directions in the hands of the poet, we are left to consider the full meaning of reversal for Greek–German relations. The Böhlendorff letter provides a helpful guide for tracing this movement of reversal, which Heidegger takes to reveal what he calls "the law of historicity" (GA 53: 170). But what is this "law"? And how does it relate to Heidegger's interpretation of both Hölderlin and Sophocles? More to our point, how does it contribute to Heidegger's own performance of poetic thinking in the Ister lectures and beyond? This law of history concerns the relation of the native and the foreign:

> The appropriation of one's own (*die Aneignung des Eigenen*) *is* only as the encounter and guest-like dialogue with the foreign (*mit dem Fremden*). Being-a-locality, being the essential locale of the homely (*Wesensart des Heimischen*) is a journeying (*Wanderschaft*) into that which is not directly bestowed upon one's own essence (*dem eigenen Wesen*), but must be learned in journeying. Yet journeying is at the same time and necessarily locality, a thoughtful, anticipatory relation to the homely .... (GA 53: 177–178/HI: 142)

If we follow the twists and turns of Heidegger's reading here, we are left to consider the essential significance of inversion and reversal for contemplating human identity and the very course of history. For Heidegger, "the law of the encounter (*Auseinandersetzung*) between the foreign and one's own is the

---

[41] William McNeill, *The Time of Life* (Albany: SUNY Press, 2006), xviii, 138.

fundamental truth of history" (GA 53: 61/HI: 49). Yet such an encounter takes the form of a necessary reversal. To understand the proper grammar of reversal, Heidegger turns to Greek tragedy to provide him with an originary insight into this law of history. What Greek tragedy teaches us is something simple yet enigmatic: "everything that is, is essentially pervaded by its counter-essence" (GA 53: 64/HI: 52). For the Ister, this means that it must flow out of its source, outward from its home and endure the journey into the foreign in order to fulfill its essential destiny. So too with the German Volk, attests Heidegger. Only by leaving its home and embarking upon a journey into the foreign – namely, into what is not of the home, the unhomely – can the Volk come into its own native and proper sense of itself. This law of coming home by way of the foreign reveals the power of Sophoclean reversal, inversion, and chiasm. Who Antigone is – the uncanniest of all that is uncanny – takes place in her enactment of a doubled and inverted movement in "a counter-turning within the essence of the human being" (GA 53: 105/HI: 85). Antigone can only come home, in this way of understanding, by virtue of her "becoming unhomely." That is what distinguishes her from her fellow human beings. Unlike her father/brother Oedipus, who is almost literally blind to the origin of his home and whose search for knowledge of his home leads him into such blindness, Antigone *knowingly* "takes it upon herself to be unhomely" (GA 53: 136/HI: 109). This decision to knowingly embrace the unhomely has to emerge from a belonging to the home or else it cannot be authentic.

It is in this sense that Heidegger can, at the same time, call Antigone herself "the purest poem" and, as the embodiment of human being in all its chiastic senses, "a catastrophe" (GA 53: 149/HI: 119). As Heidegger puts it: "The human being in its essence is a *katastrophe* – a reversal that turns it away from its own essence. Among beings, the human being is the sole catastrophe" (GA 53: 94/HI: 76). What Heidegger finds exemplary in Antigone is her willingness to embrace her being-toward-death and, in so doing, taking responsibility for the nullity that lies at the core of all stratagems of human machination. In taking upon herself this task, Antigone expresses an authentic relationship to being and thereby opens herself to the uncanniness of human being. There is something monstrous about her willingness to enter the tomb that Creon prepares for her. Yet, at the same time, we can also recognize in this bold act an opening onto a sense of the ethical. As Dennis Schmidt has argued, Antigone, as "the supreme figure of the uncanny," opens to us "the most monstrous contradiction."[42] Such a figure holds a knowledge "that is not able

---

[42] Dennis Schmidt, "The Monstrous, Catastrophe, and Ethical Life: Hegel, Heidegger, and Antigone," *Philosophy Today* 59, 1 (2015): 61–72.

to be translated into the language of philosophy with its conceptual mother tongue; rather, it belongs more properly to a poetic language." Most pointedly, however, beyond this poetic dimension, Schmidt identifies an *ethical* dimension "in which something appears that addresses us and so asks for a response from us." For Schmidt, Heidegger's reading of Antigone shows "the way we are saturated by, defined by, the questions of ethical life." Following Schmidt's lead, I want to argue for understanding Heidegger's *Antigone* in terms of an ethics of the uncanny, whereby it is the contradictory and counter-turning elements in the tragedy that raise such ethical concerns in terms of what is native and foreign, what is of the home, and what is unhomely.

Moreover, in terms of this ethical reading, I wish to argue for a reading of the uncanny (*deinos, unheimlich*) that sees it not as simply "the opposite" of what is of the home but, rather, as what intimately belongs to the home. Here we need to grasp that this uncanniness lies precisely in the belonging-together of the homely and the unhomely. As Andrew Benjamin has so persuasively claimed, "Heidegger's translation of *ta deina* as das *Unheimliche* . . . does not oppose the 'homely' (*heimisch*) to the 'unhomely' or 'uncanny' (*Unheimliche*). The point is more significant. Both are already present together."[43] An ethics of the uncanny attunes itself to Sophocles' chiastic language about the doubled nature of the human being whose own essence is turned against itself. Antigone, the character, embodies such an *ethos* since she stands as the supreme embodiment of the human being as *deinon* – the uncanny one, the one whose essence is to undertake actions against its own essence. As Heidegger puts it: "The essence of one's own (*das Eigene*) is so mysterious that it unfolds its ownmost (*eigenste*) essential wealth only from out of the supremely thoughtful acknowledgment of the foreign (*des Fremden*). This mystery of the coming-to-be-at-home (*Heimischwerden*) of the human being as historical is the poetic care of the poet of the river hymns" (GA 53: 69/HI: 55). Much as the Ister leaves its home in Donaueschingen to unfold its historical destiny of finding its home in the journey to/through the foreign, so too does the German Volk need to encounter the foreign in order to be able to return home. Their journey homeward is initiated in the poetic gesture of Hölderlin's hymn. For Heidegger, "the poet's vocation is homecoming" (GA 4: 28). At the same time, as Hölderlin well knew, such homecoming is only possible via "the experience of the foreign" that stands as the ultimate ethical ordeal that the poet must endure (GA 4: 137, 139). As he reads Antigone's fate through the lens of Hölderlinian poetic translation, Heidegger acknowledges that at the heart of what is homely lies

---

[43] Andrew Benjamin, *Place, Commonality, Judgment: Continental Philosophy and the Ancient Greeks* (London: Continuum, 2012), 101.

something profoundly unhomely, strange, foreign, and alien. In Sophocles' choral ode from *Antigone* Heidegger uncovers what I will call the tragic law of all alien homecoming – that we can only gain entry into the hearth of our home and dwelling if we first journey into what is foreign to it and thereby recognize that our home is profoundly suffused by what is alien.[44] Heidegger's poetic thinking comes to presence in this recognition of the alien element that pervades all ventures of homecoming, especially Hölderlin's. One of the most important sources for Heidegger's thinking of this law of alien homecoming is a late fragment from Hölderlin's hymn "Bread and Wine," that Heidegger turns to several times in his lecture courses and in "The Western Conversation" (GA 4: 89–93; GA 52: 189–190; GA 53; 155–164, GA 75: 140, 191).

3.4 Homeland, Colony, and the Ethical Import of the Foreign: Hölderlin's 'Bread and Wine Fragment'

Hölderlin's "Bread and Wine" elegy was written in 1800, precisely at the turn of a century, a turning that was prefigured in the Christian *parousia* whose meaning was to await the day of the gods' coming. In the poem's treatment of the Greek god Dionysus, juxtaposed against and united with the Christian Eucharist, Hölderlin unfolds the tenets of a sweeping philosophy of history. In the age of the world's night, the poet laments the forfeiture of the gods from our world, even as he celebrates the time of a profound union between gods and mortals in a *hieros gamos* experienced by the Greeks. Facing the plight of a modern age where the gods have fled, Hölderlin attests to this "time of destitution" (v. 122) while calling for an acknowledgment of a "sacred mourning" that genuinely enters into the devastation of the gods' absence, even as it sees such mourning as a preparatory attunement to a coming return of the gods upon the earth (DKV I: 290, 747–749). Heidegger cites an important fragment from this elegy (an alternate version of strophe 9) as a signature testament constituting "the law of poetic being for future poets, and the fundamental law of the history that is to be grounded by them. The historicity of history has its essence in the return to what is one's own (*zum Eigenen*), a return that can only be made as a departure into what is foreign (*als Ausfahrt in das Fremde*)" (GA 4: 95/EHP: 118 tm). The fragment reads:

> ... nemlich zu Hauß ist der Geist
> Nicht im Anfang, nicht an der Quell. Ihn zehrt die Heimat.
> Kolonie liebt, und tapfer Vergessen der Geist.
> Unsere Blumen erfreun und die Schatten unserer Wälder
> Den Verschmachteten. Fast wär der Beseeler verbrannt.

---

[44] Cf. Charles Bambach, *Of an Alien Homecoming.*

> ... namely at home is spirit
> Not at the beginning, not at the source. The homeland consumes it.
> Colony, and bold forgetting spirit loves.
> Our flowers and the shades of our woods gladden
> The one who languishes. The besouler would almost be scorched.
>   (GA 52: 190/HHR: 161–162; DKV I: 747)

Heidegger was hardly the first to recognize this law of homecoming and return in Hölderlin's poetry. Readers such as the prominent Hölderlin scholar Wolfgang Binder had argued that "Hölderlin only recognized the homeland as homeland from out of the foreign."[45] And Felix Christen, in his insightful book *Das Jetzt der Lektüre: Zur Edition und Deutung von Friedrich Hölderlins 'Ister' – Entwürfen*, has identified an impulse in Hölderlin toward what he calls "xenology" – a poetic language of the alien, the stranger, the foreigner, what the Greeks call *xenos*.[46] Within such a relation, Hölderlin's poetic idiom opens a way to understand language (and here we might think of Heidegger's own language as well) as what is a strange and alien language of what is itself strange, foreign, and other. Given such a possibility, we might pause here to consider how Heidegger's elaborate, persistent discourse on homeland, hearth, *Heimat* (and Hölderlin) can hardly be understood without these "xenological" elements. That is, we find here that Heidegger's preoccupation with *Heimat* is indissociably paired with "the experience of the foreign" that lies at its core. The "Bread and Wine" Fragment in its poetizing of spirit's journey outward places us at the crossroads and point of intersection between these two dominant themes and offers crucial insight into Heidegger's understanding of poetic dwelling.

First of all, along with the Böhlendorff letter, this Fragment stands as one of the essential sources for the way Heidegger reads the relation between ancient Greece and modern Germany, not just in Hölderlin, but in Heidegger's own thinking as well. The first line of the Fragment tells us that in the beginning, spirit (*Geist*) does not know itself; it is, rather, cut off from "the source." Moreover, within this situation of being exiled from its authentic home, spirit is besieged by a powerful force – "the homeland consumes it." But what could this mean? As Heidegger explains, "at the beginning, spirit is cast out of the homeland and thrust into an ever more futile searching ... It is the homeland itself – that which is closed off – that consumes it" (GA 4: 92/EHP: 116 tm). Yet this sense of the homeland as that which withholds itself, that which withdraws upon any attempt to enclose it within the safe boundaries of domesticity,

---

[45] Wolfgang Binder, *Hölderlin-Aufsätze* (Frankfurt: Insel, 1970), 104.

[46] Felix Christen, *Das Jetzt der Lektüre: Zur Edition und Deutung von Friedrich Hölderlins Ister-Entwürfen*. (Frankfurt: Stroemfeld, 2013), 145–148.

appears to Heidegger as "the foreign, and indeed just such a foreignness that, at the same time, lets us think of the homeland." This is precisely why spirit, which is not at home in the beginning, "loves colony." The word *colony* is of Latin origin and derives from the verb *colere* ("to cultivate"). Yet we find perhaps a deeper connection to the Greeks here since the ancient Greek word for colony is *apoikia*.[47] *Oikos* in Greek has to do with home, homeland, *Heimat* – the realm of the proper, the native, one's own. Within the Fragment, spirit's love of colony might then be read as a love of what is not at home, the unhomely, *das Unheimische*. Here, the paradox appears in poetic form that the search for what is of the home might require a journey to what is precisely not of the home, namely, the colony.

That Antigone herself is expelled from the home and, for Heidegger, comes to embody the most intense belonging to the home through such expulsion is hardly a coincidence. Rather, by finding her home in the uncanny, and fittingly accommodating herself to it, Antigone reveals herself to be "the supreme uncanny," that human being whose counter-essence turns against itself and embraces this reversal as the very signature of the proper. As Heidegger asks: "What if that which were most intrinsically unhomely, that most remote from all that is homely, were that which in itself simultaneously preserved the most intimate belonging to the homely? What if this alone, of all things, could be unhomely in the proper sense?" (GA 53: 129/HI: 104) That such a reflection on Antigone's status as "the supreme uncanny/unhomely" takes place in a lecture course focused on the riverine peregrinations of the Ister proves perhaps difficult to grasp. And yet we can find an enduring connection here in the journeying of the river from the source to its mouth – and, more than this, in its seeming reversal where the Ister "appears/to travel backwards" ("The Ister," vv. 41–42). It is in the river's poetic course of journeying that we find the enactment of a Hölderlinian *ethos* of dwelling, one that carries out a poetology of origin and end, of arrival, and of what is to come. As Heidegger himself puts it: "Anfang bliebt als Ankunft" / "Beginning remains as arrival" (GA 4: 171/EHP: 195). Here we find one of the great insights of Heidegger's Hölderlin writings: The beginning is something that abides only as long as it is coming. "Origin" does not exist as a static antecedent to whatever comes after; on the contrary, origin lies ahead of us, as that to which we must open ourselves if we wish to enter into its originary power. As Heidegger reminds us in *On the Way to Language*: "Herkunft aber bleibt stets Zukunft"/"But provenance always remains as that which is to come" (GA 12: 91).

---

[47] Franco Montinari, *The Brill Dictionary of Ancient Greek* (Leiden: Brill, 2018), 250; Menge-Güthling, *Griechisch-Deutsch* (Berlin: Langenscheidts, 1957), 482.

The Ister's origin lies in the Greek name Istros and the Roman designation of the lower half of the river as Ister, with the upper half being named Danuvius. As Hölderlin takes upon himself the poetic task of "naming," he will combine both names into one whereby this singular name "Ister" expresses a Heraclitean identity-in-difference. Not only is the spatial division into upper and lower halves now unified, but Hölderlin also unifies them in a temporal sense by finding an underlying kinship between the ancient Greek Istros and the modern German Donau (Danube) by way of their reversal. Hölderlin draws upon the significance of naming in his own reading of the Greeks. Greek tragedy abounds with the ironic – and portentous – play upon names and naming. Antigone's name puns upon her embrace of death rather than birth (anti-genesis); Pentheus, in Euripides' play *The Bacchae*, refuses to acknowledge the name of "the Stranger" in the drama (who is the god Dionysus) and because of this willful arrogance learns the hidden etymological significance of his own name "Pentheus" (from the Greek *penthos*, "the one who suffers"). Beyond this, we find similar reversals with names in Euripides' *Hippolytus* (where *lyein* signifies loosening or dissolution by horses, *hippoi*) and paradigmatically in Oedipus' confusion as to the origin of his own name (that combines/conflates *oidein* – "swell" + *pous* "foot" with the Greek roots *oid-* and *eid-* "to know" + "to see"). For Hölderlin, the naming of the Donau (Danube) as "The Ister" serves as a bold challenge to Germans to recognize their relation to the ancient world, to the river as the source of their destiny, to the foreign as essential to their native identity. This phenomenon of naming is to serve the Germans in at least two distinct senses. Firstly, through the act of renaming what is familiar to them under a different designation, Hölderlin attempts a reversal that strives to spur Germans out of their stupor by calling for a poetic attunement to a new relation to the gods who dwell there but are hardly acknowledged. Secondly, the poem itself is to serve as the enactment of the river's own archetypal movement of departure and return, *Ausflug* and *Rückkehr*, so that the encounter with the foreign poetized there will bring the *Volk* into an authentic experience of their native homeland.

This poetic *ethos* of dwelling that recognizes the importance of the foreign for one's own native endowment will prove decisive for Heidegger's own thinking. In the Ister lectures, Heidegger reads the apparent reversal of the river's course as that which "intimates the mysterious concealment of the intertwining relations toward the foreign and one's own" (GA 53: 178/HI: 143). There Heidegger relates that poetic dwelling depends on acknowledging the mysterious pull of the river's countermovement in such a way that we also recognize the alterity of what lies counter to us as an essential element in our dwelling. This can not simply involve the arrogation of the other for our own task. As

Heidegger puts it, "The relation to the foreign is never a mere taking over of the Other." Here Heidegger's framing of the law of alien homecoming underlines just how necessary the other is for our own native identity. One might even argue that in this form, Heidegger offers something like an ethical insight into the heart of human dwelling:

> For only where the foreign is known and acknowledged in its essential oppositional character does there exist the possibility of a passage through the foreign, and thereby the possibility of a return home into one's own, and thereby that which is one's own itself. (GA 53: 68/HI: 54)

But still the question persists – does this journey into the foreign by the native sojourner truly involve a recognition of the foreignness of the foreign? Or does the foreign here merely serve as a way station for spirit's own homeward bound wayfaring? In his *Remembrance* lectures, Heidegger offers us a puzzling response:

> The sojourn (*Aufenthalt*) in the foreign and the learning of the foreign, not for the sake of the foreign, but for the sake of one's own, demands that perseverant standing one's ground that no longer thinks of one's own. (GA 52: 190/ HHR: 162 tm)

In the Ister lectures, Heidegger returns to a reading of the "Bread and Wine" Fragment about spirit's love of colony and bold forgetting and offers us some hints toward an understanding of the foreign. There he explicitly states: "Bold forgetting" is the knowledge and mindful courage to experience the foreign, an experiencing that, in the foreign, steadfastly gives thought to one's own. The boldness of forgetting in the love of colony is the readiness, while in the foreign, to learn from the foreign for the sake of what is one's own . . . ." (GA 53: 165/HI: 132)

On several occasions during these lectures, Heidegger will emphasize that the journey to the foreign, like the translation of Greek into German, is "for the sake of" the native, the proper, one's own (GA 53: 80, 154, 165–166, 168). Venturing into the colony, then, must be understood as "the decisive act of return to the home" for the sake of what is one's own. And here we find notes of the selfsame privileging of the native that serves to undermine, or at least challenge, the thinking of a poetic ethics of dwelling that draws inspiration from Hölderlin. Ultimately, we are left with some troubling questions about Heidegger's privileging of the native within his work. During the early years of National Socialist rule as Heidegger gets caught up in the feverish patriotism of the day, he writes in his Black Notebooks of "the Germans" and attests that "the taking possession of the distant decree of the inception waits upon them alone" (GA 94: 95). Moreover, in these very notebooks, Heidegger remarks: "Only the German can say and poetize being in a new, originary way" (GA 94: 27).

At the same time, we find in the Ister lectures profound philosophical insights into questions about dwelling, homecoming, *ethos*, and the tragic situation of human beings. Heidegger's focus on the tragic dimension of the uncanny homelessness that threatens our sojourn upon the earth places it at the very heart of any authentic account of poetic dwelling. There is no question but that for Heidegger "the finding and appropriating of one's own remains what is most difficult" (GA 53: 179, 171/HI: 143, 137). This form of dwelling poetically confronts us as what is most difficult precisely because "dwelling itself, being homely, is the becoming homely of a being unhomely." We can identify here an uncanny paradox in Heidegger's unfolding of the uncanny, especially where it confronts the privileging of a German *Sonderweg* or special path at the expense of other nations, languages, peoples, and ways of dwelling. We could at this juncture turn to an extended analysis of what both Peter Trawny and Donatella Di Cesare have termed Heidegger's "beyng-historical" anti-Semitism and "metaphysical-racism," respectively.[48] Such an analysis would necessarily have to take account of Heidegger's rebarbative comments about Jews in the Black Notebooks, but here there is not the space to address this in any depth. What we need to bring to notice, rather, is the tension in Heidegger's writings between the attunement to an *ethos* of poetic dwelling *and* his commitment to a destinal politics of exclusion that places the Germans as the sole nation and people capable of "saving the West" (GA 13: 16; GA 55: 69, 108; GA 80: 693). On the one hand, Heidegger identifies a historical-destinal singularity in the German Volk based on their consanguineous bond to the ancient Greeks, an identification that has brought with it a fatal political legacy. On the other hand, Heidegger stands as perhaps the most significant philosopher of modernity in reclaiming the poetic legacy of thinking necessary to undertake what the task of philosophy requires. He does so not only through his reading and engagement with specific poets such as Hölderlin, Rilke, Trakl, George, Hebel, or Celan, but perhaps more significantly in the way he performs his own singular kind of poetic thinking that opens up language to us in a new and originary way. This is the burden of reading Heidegger today – to acknowledge his political and racial-ideological missteps while not abandoning his powerful insights into the plight of a modernity left homeless by the overreach of its technological surge for mastery over the earth. To address some of the ways Heidegger does this, we will need to look at his postwar writings on technology, instrumental thinking, and their effects on our relationship to language – and/as poetic dwelling.

---

[48] Peter Trawny, "Typen des Seinsgeschichtlichen Antisemitismus," *Heidegger und der Mythos der jüdischen Weltverschwörung*, (Frankfurt: Klostermann, 2014), 31–56 and Donatella DiCesare, *Heidegger, Die Juden, Die Shoah* (Frankfurt: Klostermann, 2016), 256–262.

4 The Later Heidegger on Poetic Dwelling

4.1 The Transition Year: 1946

The fallout from Germany's devastating losses in World War II would leave a permanent mark upon the German landscape. It would also have a strong effect on Heidegger, even if it took him several years to genuinely work through what the war's impact would mean – philosophically and personally. On the day the war ended, May 8, 1945, Heidegger wrote in his notebooks:

> The War at an end, nothing changed, nothing new, on the contrary.
> What has already long endured must now emerge in an evident way …
> The *devastation* (*Verwüstung*) – that it goes on further. (GA 77: 241)

After the bitter defeat and the coming to account of "the question of German guilt" in the Nuremberg Trials (1946), Heidegger was forced to confront charges of collaboration with the Nazi regime by French military authorities and the Freiburg faculty. As a result, he loses his right to teach for five years and undergoes a grave psychological crisis in 1946 that threatens him to the core. When he emerges from this crisis, he begins to write some of the most important essays within his corpus – "The Letter on Humanism," "What are Poets For?," and "The Verdict of Anaximander." Moreover, as a way to address the devastation of the epoch, Heidegger writes that "In the world epoch of the world's night the abyss of the world must be experienced and withstood" (GA 5: 270). During the next several years, Heidegger would embark upon one of his most important contributions to an understanding of the modern age in *The Bremen Lectures* (1949). There Heidegger would develop his critique of global technology and instrumental thinking as *das Gestell* or "positionality" where all entities are positioned as useful items there for our consumption, ever on standing reserve, awaiting to be produced, ordered, dispatched, and digitally catalogued as available inventory for future retrieval. Foremost among Heidegger's concerns here is the way such positionality configures the human being's approach to language, turning it into yet another instrument on call to allow for a more thorough and wide-ranging control over the entities at our disposal. Already in the 1940s–50s, Heidegger was attuned to the multiple ways cybernetics (what we would now term "AI") forms and informs our thinking, the way it "steers" (from the Greek *kybernesis*, the art of steering) and mobilizes the power of technology to make available a pervasive uniformity of measure whereby measure itself loses its alien character as what lies beyond our ken to become a functional tool of calculative conformity. As Heidegger put it in a late seminar at Le Thor:

> In positionality (*Gestell*) the human being is challenged to comport itself
> corresponding to exploitation and consumption; the relation to exploitation
> and consumption compels the human being to *be* in this relation. The human
> being does not hold technology in its hand. It is technology's plaything. In
> this situation there reigns a consummate forgetfulness of being,
> a consummate concealment of being. Cybernetics becomes a replacement
> for philosophy and poetry. (GA 15: 369–370/FS: 62–62)

During the 1950s, Heidegger would draw on his critique of technology outlined
in The Bremen Lectures and bring it into conversation with the power of
originary *poiesis*. As Heidegger reminds us there, *poiesis* is less the product
of a human "making" than it is a bringing-forth from out of itself that expresses
the Greek sense of *physis*. In "The Question Concerning Technology,"
Heidegger explicitly states that *poiesis* is not only artistic-poetic crafting,
making, designing, but a "bringing-forth" into presence. There Heidegger
goes on to stress that "*physis* is indeed *poiesis* in the supreme sense" (GA 7:
12). In Hölderlin's "As on a Holiday . . .," *physis* comes to presence not in the
sense of objective presence but as a presence that offers hints of that which is
absent. In its opening image of a field left abandoned during an evening storm,
Hölderlin conveys the force of nature's withdrawal in the distant thunder that
still rumbles from afar. Poetic revelation differs essentially from the way
technology brings forth its products by drawing our attention to the phenomenon of concealment rather than by trying to force concealment into presence
through the impositioning of its own demands. The very program of such
positionality cuts off any authentic experience of what *poiesis* means for our
way of dwelling. In 1951, Heidegger writes three separate essays that speak to
the genuine sense of *poiesis* as a form of dwelling, essays written to address the
situation of loss, devastation, forfeiture, and abandonment that pervade the West
in the cybernetic age of production, essays that speak to our sense of detachment
from the earth upon which we build and dwell. These three essays – "Building
Dwelling Thinking," ". . . poetically dwells the human being. . .," and "On
Contemporary Poetry" (GA 7: 145–164; 189–208 and GA 80: 1033–1040) –
offer genuinely helpful insight into Heidegger's postwar expressions of poetic
thinking. Each of these essays was delivered as a public address and each offers
a good sense of how Heidegger wished to communicate this new kind of poetic
thinking to his contemporaries. In some preliminary remarks to one of his public
addresses from 1951, Heidegger poses a direct question: "What can we do to
save the poem from its homelessness?" (GA 16: 470; GA 80: 1039). In this last
section, I want to offer readings of the first two essays to provide a better sense
of Heidegger's pressing question in the very different political landscape of
postwar Germany. Let us turn first to "Building Dwelling Thinking."

4.2 Building Dwelling Thinking

In a world where everything is a resource, where language itself takes the form of a commodity, and where the places we live and dwell become listings that are catalogued, displayed, packaged, and defined as "real estate" (from its Latin roots – "the standing thing" – *res* + *stare*), how might we learn to dwell more authentically? As Heidegger turns once again in 1951 to rethinking the genuine impoverishment of our dwelling, he is confronted by pressing social, economic, and political issues. Within the newly formed German Federal Republic, there persists a severe housing shortage brought on by the devastation incurred by Allied air bombings. Millions of Germans had lost their homes and were forced to resettle in makeshift living quarters. As a response to this postwar situation, the architect Otto Bartning convened a series of *Gespräche* (conversations) in Darmstadt to address the issue of "reconstruction" in a country literally torn in half by the predations of war. In a fascinating study that situates Heidegger's essay "Building Dwelling Thinking" in terms of this crisis, Tobias Keiling argues that it is crafted as a response to Bartning's notion of building as a "basic activity of the human" and to the conference's overall theme that "homelessness is the plight of our time."[49] Keiling stresses that for Heidegger "the notion of dwelling functions as a basic term for human life" and, moreover, that "*before* we can engage in any merely ontic activity relating to dwelling," we need to undergo "an encounter with poetry." Following Keiling, I will argue that dwelling itself is nothing less than the way human beings *are* upon the earth. Dwelling, then, can hardly be designated as one activity among many other possible ones; it stands, rather, as the fundamental human way to be. Yet, for Heidegger, dwelling cannot properly occur unless we have already engaged in a different way of thinking – a poetic thinking of our relation to building and dwelling.

"Building Dwelling Thinking" offers both an analysis of the prevailing situation of homelessness in Germany and a challenge to alter our relation to the reigning mode of thinking about such homelessness. The genuine problem of homelessness, Heidegger tells us, cannot be addressed by simply building more houses for those who are without shelter. What matters, rather, is to ponder anew two questions that might offer a different path into the very meaning of building itself as a human activity. Heidegger asks:

1. What is dwelling?
2. In what way does building belong to dwelling? (GA 7: 147/PLT: 145 tm)

---

[49] Tobias Keiling, "Dwelling after 1945: Heidegger among the Architects," in Ingo Farin & Jeff Malpas, eds, *Heidegger and the Human* (Albany: SUNY Press, 2022), 325–351, here 341–343.

Within our usual ways of thinking we have the possibility of dwelling only if we first engage in building a place to dwell. According to this logic, building constitutes a fundamental prerequisite for dwelling as a means-ends proposition. Here we find Heidegger at odds with Otto Bartning's aim of seeing building and architecture as a way of "overcoming homelessness."[50] Architecture alone can hardly address this question in an originary way. Rather, Heidegger wants to show that "Building is not merely a means and a way toward dwelling; building is in itself already a dwelling" (GA 7: 148/PLT: 146). To pursue the connection between building and dwelling further, Heidegger turns to language, specifically etymology – although he is not unmindful of the dangers involved in a servile fidelity to "word research" as offering scholarly "proof" of anything. What he seeks, rather, is to unfold the concealed force of the most elemental words and bring them to an intimacy with thinking. He does so in the essay's focus on the etymological roots of the German words for building and dwelling – *Bauen* and *Wohnen*.

In Old High German, the word for building is *buan*, which originally means "to dwell." This signifies – "to remain, to abide in an abode (*sich aufhalten*)" (GA 7: 148–149/PLT: 146–147 tm). *Buan*, like *Bauen*, reaches back to the German verb for *being* which, in its forms "I am" and "you are" (*Ich bin, du bist*) means "I dwell," "you dwell." As Heidegger puts it: "The way in which you are and I am, the manner in which we humans *are* upon the earth is *Buan*, dwelling. To be human means to be on the earth as a mortal. It means: to dwell." Yet in the way we comport ourselves upon the earth, driven hither and fro in our ceaseless excursions, we have lost a sense of *Bauen* as dwelling. Within our epoch, we have fallen into oblivion regarding the originary sense of dwelling. Moreover, as part of our inattentive and dispersive experience of the world, "dwelling is never thought as the fundamental trait of the human being." Hence, Heidegger raises the question – "What, however, constitutes the essence of dwelling?" (GA 7: 150). Again, Heidegger finds the proper path for addressing such a question in the history of the Old Saxon word *wuon* – with its Gothic cognate *wunian*, which has to do with one's abode, the place where one abides and flourishes. He then goes on to show that the fundamental trait of dwelling lies in "protecting" (*Schonen*), which is another form of "caring for" things. But how does dwelling relate to building in the way we strive to protect and nurture the world we inhabit?

As a way to address this question, Heidegger turns to a kind of building that brings together an understanding of things in their relation to *das Gestell* and *das Geviert*, to positionality and to the fourfold at once. As his iconic

---

[50] Otto Bartning, ed., *Darmstädter Gespräche: Mensch und Raum* (Darmstadt: Neue Darmstädter Verlagsanstalt, 1952) and Karsten Harries, "In Search of Home," 101–120.

exemplar, he chooses the Old Bridge in Heidelberg (die Karlsbrücke) that spans the Neckar River and brings together its opposite banks into a unity that allows for, and indeed invites, the polarities of such tension. Hölderlin poetized the Karlsbrücke in his ode "Heidelberg" that sang of the bridge as the site for the appearance of "the radiance and lure of far-distant places."[51] For Hölderlin, the bridge serves as the gathering site for landscape, humans, gods, and heavenly sky in such a way that each element of the gathering is simultaneously preserved in its singularity even as such singularity ultimately rests in its elemental interconnection with the others. It is hardly a rash leap of judgment to find in these poetic allusions a source for Heidegger's own difficult and challenging notion of the fourfold. For Heidegger, the bridge is nothing less than a thing that gathers the fourfold in such a way that it lets the bridge be what it essentially is. Perhaps here we can find a point of comparison for placing the two notions of the fourfold and positionality into conversation.

Let us first take the bridge. As the structure that roots itself in the earth and vaults upward toward the sky, while simultaneously bringing two banks together, the bridge shows both vertical and horizontal forces of union and separation. Here earth, sky, divinities, and mortals come into a tensional unity; to think one is to think all together in a fundamental relation. This is what enables world and grants dwelling; but dwelling cannot happen on its own. Settlement? Perhaps. Residence? Yes. But dwelling requires an attunement to the world that is bound up with poetic thinking, a thinking that takes the measure of our dwelling in a poetic way, which, in turn, enables us to build. Building lets the fourfold come forth. Here again, Heidegger does not insert the human into the project of building as the one who assertively builds, constructs, designs, and implements. On the contrary, such building lets being unfold as a way of gathering the human being into the fourfold of sky, earth, and divinities. Here the human being does not take center stage but attunes itself to the way each element of the four allows for the interplay of all elements to emerge. Let us return to the example of the Old Bridge. In "Building Dwelling Thinking," Heidegger compares the different ways in which the bridge gathers and the Autobahn disperses the elemental gathering of the fourfold. Neither the bridge nor the Autobahn are designed as places of residence. In their openness to the sky, each stands there as a structural entity built to enable passageway through the world. And yet in their relation to the topos of dwelling, each stands in contrast to the other. The bridge gathers the earth as a landscape, encompassing the river that passes beneath it, letting the

---

[51] Friedrich Hölderlin, DKV I: 242. The translation is from Michael Hamburger, *Hölderlin: Selected Poems and Fragments*, 51.

river flow onwards on its own course even as, at the same time, it allows for humans to traverse it above. The Autobahn, on the other hand, appears everywhere across the landscape without belonging to it in any essential way. The bridges built across the Autobahn reflect this indifference to place, site, topos. As Heidegger put it, "The Autobahn bridge is fastened into the network of routes calculated for the greatest possible speed in long-distance transport" (GA 7: 155/ PLT: 152 tm). It does not let any gathering of the fourfold appear. Instead it imposes its structural demands upon its environment and becomes another integral component in the organization and distribution of space according to the calculus of positionality. Here in the juxtaposition of the Old Bridge and the Autobahn Bridge, Heidegger underlines the adversarial relation of *Gestell* and *Geviert*, where the fourfold allows for interplay, conjuncture, and intimative gathering whereas the gathering (*Ge-*) of positionality (*stellen*) merely requisitions (*bestellen*), erects (*erstellen*), produces (*herstellen*), represents (*vorstellen*), and distorts (*verstellen*) entities so that they might be stored, catalogued, and stockpiled (*Bestand*) as "resources."

Foremost amongst the resources that are stockpiled and surveyed is the human being. Here, the human gets repartitioned so that body parts can now be digitally monitored as available inventory for future retrieval. Organs get transplanted; seminal fluids are matched to prospective eggs in Petri dishes; body parts are replaced through titanium appendages. Ineluctably, the human sphere gives itself over to the positionality that positions us on the model of what Theodore Kisiel has called "synthetic composit(ion)ing" – "the synthetic compositing of binary-digital logic [that] maps out the grand artifact of the technological infrastructure that networks the entire globe of our planet Earth."[52] What comes to reign with *das Gestell* is "the gathering unity of all ways of setting into place, positioning, positing (*Stellens*)" (GA 15: 366/FS: 60). As Heidegger goes on to say, where the positing of *Gestell* "holds sway, it drives out every other possibility of revealing. Above all, positionality conceals that revealing which in the sense of *poiesis*, lets what presences come forth into appearance" (GA 7: 28/BW: 332). It is crucial to note here that *das Gestell* is not something that humans control, direct, steer, or have dominion over. On the contrary, it is positionality itself that both posits and positions the human being within the way it reveals itself. As Heidegger notes in "The Question Concerning Technology": "Positionality (*Ge-stell*) means the gathering together of that positing (*Stellen*) that positions (*stellt*) the human being, i.e., challenges it forth, to reveal the actual, in the mode of requisitioning (*bestellen*), as standing-reserve (*Bestand*). As the one who is challenged forth

---

[52] Theodore Kisiel, "Synthetic Composit(ion)ing (*Ge-stell*)," in Mark Wrathall, ed., *Heidegger Lexicon* (Cambridge: Cambridge University Press, 2020), 710–718.

in this way, the human being stands within the essential realm of positionality" (GA 7: 24–25/BW: 329). As John Loscerbo reminds us, "*Gestell* means 'a way of revealing,' *not* however a manner of human revealing but a *Sich Entbergen* (self-revealing)."[53] That is why Heidegger can say that "*Gestell* means the way of revealing that holds sway in the essence of modern technology and that is itself nothing technological" (GA 7: 21/BW: 325).

If our contemporary way of building is caught up in the manifold ways of construction, organization, planning, and fabrication of modern residences, then our possibilities for dwelling wind up being severely compromised. Building does not precede dwelling as its causal prerequisite. No mere assemblage of concrete, steel, wood, or glass can provide us with an adequate dwelling place. Dwelling requires and demands, rather, a different way of thinking, a poetic thinking attuned to the Heraclitean play of revelation and/as concealment. Within such a transformed way of thinking, we come to understand truth not as the correspondence to what is present before us, but as an event of withdrawal and departure that thinks the ground (*Grund*) of things as abyss (*Ab-grund*). If in Fragment B123 Heraclitus can say "Being (*physis*) loves to hide," Heidegger thinks this even more cryptically as "Emergence (from out of self-concealment) grants its favor to self-concealment" (GA 7: 279). This same power of self-concealment will be forgotten, however, in our technologically driven push toward construction of buildings and in our occupation of such buildings as our "residence." "Building Dwelling Thinking" casts its question about the possibility of building as a question about poetic dwelling and poetic thinking. It asks us to reconsider how we move about in our world as an assemblage of objects that can be accumulated, displayed, consumed, and deployed to fulfill our own designs. It gives thought to the very sense of things not as the bearers of properties, as substances attached to accidents, or as formed matter. It asks, rather, that we experience the thing as inherently relational, as that which gestures out beyond itself. As Andrew Mitchell explains: "The thing begins outside of itself and this already disrupts any idea of a stable or fixed presence. The thing is not present to itself, but already outside and ahead of itself."[54] Things gather around them a world of relations that enable us to dwell; they do so by "thinging" – that is, "in thinging (*dingend*) the thing lets earth and sky, lets divinities and mortals abide. Abiding (*verweilend*), the thing brings the four, in their remoteness, near to one another" (GA 7: 179/PLT: 177 tm). The fourfold enables the thinging of the thing, even as the thing gathers the fourfold within its way of thinging.

---

[53] John Loscerbo, *Being and Technology* (The Hague: Martinus Nijhoff, 1981), 146.

[54] Andrew Mitchell, *The Fourfold: Reading the Late Heidegger* (Evanston: Northwestern University Press, 2015), 15.

It might be tempting to see the two dominant ways of revealing in our modern epoch – the singularity that attaches to the thing as it gathers *das Geviert* and the replaceability that characterizes *das Gestell* – as two separate and distinct realms. Here we could sequester the fourfold from positionality and place each in its appropriate realm. Yet for Heidegger, there is no such easy compartmentalization. As Andrew Mitchell puts it: "Heidegger insists on the tension between the two, between the thing and the standing reserve, positionality and the fourfold, *Gestell* and *Geviert*, the danger and what saves. In sum, it is not that there is something salvatory somewhere apart from an external danger that we happen to have fallen into. Rather, Heidegger thinks the danger and the saving together."[55] For Heidegger, insofar as "the danger is beyng itself, it is nowhere and everywhere. It has no place" (GA 79: 72/BFL: 68). Moreover, "The danger is the epoch of beyng, essencing as positionality." In the epoch of such danger, beings are caught in this binary tension between *Gestell* as "the challenging-forth" or *Herausforderung* of all beings and *Geviert* where, in the mode of thinging, things "bring forth" (*Hervorbringen*) world wherein the gathering of the four happens. In our lived world of the uniformity and sameness of objects, we find the well-worn tracks of conformity to a way of organizing that transforms things into commodities even as in so doing it deforms them so as to make them unrecognizable as things capable of gathering the play of the fourfold. The real danger here, Heidegger tells us, is "not simply that it imperils the human being in its relation to itself and to everything that is," but that it blocks or obstructs any other way of revealing than that adjured by *Gestell* (GA 7: 28). Within this epoch of *Gestell*, there reigns the implacable onslaught of the abandonment of being.

Yet how should the human being comport itself within this destining of being's withdrawal? What kind of *ethos* would seem most fitting, most proper, in our current situation? In his first Duino Elegy, Rainer Maria Rilke expresses something of this sense of human displacement:

> . . . and the clever animals already notice,
> how little at home we are
> in the interpreted world./
> . . . und die findigen Tiere merken es schon,
> dass wir nicht sehr verlässlich zu Haus sind
> in der gedeuteten Welt.[56]

---

[55] Andrew Mitchell, "The Bremen Lectures," in Francois Raffoul & Eric Nelson, eds., *Bloomsbury Companion to Heidegger* (London: Bloomsbury, 2013), 248.

[56] Rainer Maria Rilke, *Duino Elegies: Bilingual Edition*, trans. Edward Snow (New York: North Point Press, 2000), 4–5.

In his "What Are Poets For?" essay, Heidegger will note how in comparison with his contemporaries, "Rilke experiences the destitution of the age more clearly" (GA 5: 274). Yet Heidegger goes beyond Rilke's diagnosis of destitution to show how "mortals are still not in possession of their essence." Our technological epoch has itself precluded any experience of such possession. The gods have fled; the world's night prevails. Any trace of the sacred has been blocked and occluded by the unrelenting pulse of technological dominance. Are there mortals still capable of "recognizing the danger that assails the human being?" To address this question, Heidegger cites the opening lines from Hölderlin's hymn "Patmos":

> But where there is danger,
> There grows also that which saves. (GA 5: 294)

In "Building Dwelling Thinking," Heidegger addresses the relation of danger and saving in terms of human dwelling and thinks dwelling, in turn, as an abiding with things that preserves the fourfold in the human sojourn upon the earth. It is to poets that Heidegger turns to help him think this relation anew, for it is poets like Rilke and Hölderlin who give word to the plight of homelessness that threatens the human being. It is precisely such homelessness – when thought in its proper sense – that serves as "the sole summons that calls mortals into their dwelling" (GA 7: 164/PLT: 161). Danger and saving belong together. For Heidegger, it is poets who most powerfully recognize the danger – and, in so doing, it is they who understand the indissoluble bond that connects them. Yet it would be amiss to suggest that the coupling of danger and saving can be addressed only through poetizing. Such a question also demands a thinking of this bond between danger and saving, one that involves a poetic thinking. Heidegger offers one of the best expressions of such thinking in his essay "... poetically dwells the human being."

4.3 Poetic Dwelling as Poetic Thinking

In "... poetically dwells the human being ...," Heidegger offers a kind of bookend for his analysis of building in "Building Dwelling Thinking" and he does so by thinking building in terms of poetic dwelling. But the dwelling (*Wohnen*) that Heidegger thinks here is not one whereby we read poetic verse or write quatrains in order to better dwell. Poetic dwelling involves a more attuned relation to the very possibility and promise of what such a dwelling entails. Again, Heidegger turns to a verse from Hölderlin's late poem "In lovely blueness ..." as a way to find such attunement: "When Hölderlin speaks of dwelling he has in mind the fundamental character of human Dasein. However, he catches sight of the "poetic" from out of the relationship to this dwelling, essentially understood" (GA 7: 193/PLT: 215 tm). Drawing upon Hölderlin's insights, Heidegger now rethinks what such a poetic dwelling signifies. First of all, it cannot mean that in all our modes of dwelling something poetic comes to the fore. Rather, he claims, "the verse '... poetically dwells the human being ...' says: poetizing first and foremost lets dwelling be dwelling. Poetizing is, properly understood, letting dwell." But Heidegger goes further to show that the way to attain to a dwelling place is through building, whereby poetizing – understood as that which lets us dwell – is to be grasped as a kind of building. Again, here we see Heidegger taking up some of the same themes as in his earlier lectures on Hölderlin in the "Remembrance" and "Ister" courses. Yet if there Heidegger spoke often of *Heimat, Heimkehr*, and *Heimischwerden* (homeland, homecoming, and becoming homely) to emphasize an attachment to the German soil and, through such a connection, to language as an intimate element of poetic thinking, the Heidegger of the late forties and early fifties takes a new path. The term "Heimat" goes underground as it were and instead of the politically charged discourse of homeland, in the postwar environment of the Nuremberg Trials, the Allied Occupation, and his own teaching ban, Heidegger now deploys a new set of terms centered around building, poetizing, homelessness, sojourn, and dwelling. There persists, however, the same focus on *ethos* as "the abode, the dwelling place, the open region in which the human being dwells" (GA 9: 354/PM: 269). In SS 1944, Heidegger will read *ethos* as "dwelling (*Wohnung*), sojourn (*Aufenthalt*)" and grasp it in terms of an "'ethics,' thought here broadly and essentially, [that] seeks to understand how the human abides in this sojourn amidst beings and in this way maintains and holds itself" (GA 55: 214). Heidegger even goes so far as to say here that "self-understanding in terms of *ethos*, the knowledge thereof, is 'ethics'" (GA 55: 206). Yet we also know that in "The Letter on Humanism," Heidegger was quick to detach himself from providing any kind of an ordinary "ethics" as a corrective to *Being and Time* or to the demand by Karl Jaspers that Germany confront its essential guilt for "that which happened."[57] Heidegger in fact understands the longing for a rules-based form of ethics with its strictures and directions as bound up with the same kind of gathering and planning activities that pervade the world of technology. Hence, Heidegger refuses to accede to this demand of *Gestell* to furnish a technologically constructed "ought" for the epoch of the world wars. Instead, Heidegger turns to Fragment 119 of Heraclitus – *ethos anthropoi daimon* – and translates it in his own inimitable

---

[57] This is the way that Paul Celan refers to the crimes and exterminations in the camps of National Socialism during World War II, *Gesammelte Werke* (Frankfurt: Suhrkamp, 1986), III: 186.

way as "Der (geheure) Aufenthalt ist dem Menschen das Offene für die Anwesung des Gottes (des Un-geheuren)." In William McNeill's translation from the German: "The (familiar) abode for humans is the open region for the presencing of god (the un-familiar one)" (GA 9: 356/PM: 271).

Heidegger sets out here to free our thinking from the *Gestell* of "applied ethics" and its constellation of themes centered around thetic human control to think what he calls an "originary ethics" not grounded in rules or codes but attuned, rather, to the thinking of being. Like Nietzsche, Heidegger seeks to break with the precepts of morality to think of a human relation to the world without god or metaphysics. Such an originary ethics thinks of the ethicality of ethics as having to do with the openness of being and of the human sojourn within the world as a comportment toward, or an *ethos* of, dwelling. Such an ethics cannot be calculated, nor can it be measured by results and outcomes. This originary ethics focuses on *ethos* as a form of dwelling in an epoch where the very possibility of dwelling is threatened by the onset of a profound homelessness marked by "the abandonment of beings by being" (GA 9: 339). Moreover, Heidegger's poetic thinking here thinks the dwelling of the human being in terms of originary ethics and our ensuing responsibility to comport ourselves in attunement with being's way of manifesting in an open relation. We find ourselves in such an open relation when we attend to language as the proper place of our dwelling, the site of our sojourn upon the earth that reveals our poetic relation to being. But entry into our poetic dwelling does not come of itself. It must first be learned. Our very relation to the poetic character of our dwelling has been so occluded by the machinations of *Gestell* that we have become estranged from our own way of being. Strangers to ourselves, we have become unsettled in our settlements, dispossessed of our habitat, cast adrift by the alien promise of technological mastery over our environs. And yet what matters to Heidegger in his thinking of poetic dwelling is precisely an openness to the alien, the foreign, and the unhomely/uncanny. We saw earlier in our discussion of Sophocles' *Antigone* how dwelling in the uncanny, the foreign, and the strange constitutes an essential part of our being-at-home and that our lack of attunement to such a strange form of dwelling places us at odds with our ownmost capacity for dwelling poetically. But are we capable of embracing that which is alien as we set about on our sojourn to secure our proper home? And would a poetical form of dwelling ever be something that could be "secured"?

Heidegger is quite clear about our current state of dwelling: The human being dwells upon the earth today – but not poetically (GA 13: 216). And he goes on to add that "the 'unpoetic' names the non-essence of the poetic, that which is uncanny (*Unheimliches*) in it" (GA 13: 218–219). What distinguishes this uncanny, unpoetic way of dwelling is how the human being "seizes upon a measure from an earth disfigured by human machination." But Heidegger's urgent call to heed Hölderlin's poetic word bespeaks a quite different kind of measure, a poetic measure, whose metric and *metron* can hardly be metered on the instruments of computation.

4.3.1 The Poetic Measure of Dwelling

Delivered at first as a lecture at the Bühlerhöhe spa in the northern Black Forest, "... poetically dwells the human being ..." takes up a reading of Hölderlin as a way to address the question of homelessness and the loss of any sense of a proper measure for dwelling. Ten years earlier in one of his Black Notebooks entries, Heidegger had written: "Where the measureless (*Masslose*) reigns, "measurements" (*Ausmasse*) become a nullity because their enhanced succession makes every measure (*Mass*) forgotten. The forgottenness is necessary in order to maintain the unconditional essencelessness of beings. "Goals" are achieved even while no one wants to achieve a goal" (GA 96: 254). In the Bühlerhöhe address, Heidegger will complement the thinking of poetic measure with his earlier Darmstadt talk on "Building Dwelling Thinking" and say: "Poetizing, as the authentic measuring-out (*ermessen*) of the dimension of dwelling, is the originary form of building" (GA 7: 206). But how does Heidegger understand poetizing as an *originary* form of building? And what would it mean to find a measure for dwelling in the poetic? To address such questions for Heidegger involves at least three critical realms that need to be thought together and yet separately as well.

Firstly, Heidegger acknowledges the contemporary situation of Germany that provides the backdrop for his talk – namely, the threat of coming winter, shortages of fuel for heat, and what he calls the affliction of the housing shortage. But that is hardly the decisive element here. Rather, what afflicts our dwelling is the epochal sense of a pervasive homelessness that is of ontological rather than ontic provenance, the sense that we live in an age where, as Hölderlin put it, "names for the holy are deficient" (*"es fehlen heilige Nahmen"*) (DKV I: 245). It is as a response to this deficit that Heidegger offers a reading of a late poem of Hölderlin's, "In lovely blueness." That Heidegger would turn to a poet to address questions of dwelling tells us much about his own distance from the reigning professional disciples of architecture, urban planning, or economics that expressed a quite different *ethos* of dwelling. Indeed he makes clear in his essay that "our unpoetic dwelling, its inability to take the measure, comes forth from out a strange excess (*Übermass*) of frantic measuring and calculating" (GA 7: 207). The third feature prominent in Heidegger's reading, apart from his sensitivity to the contemporary plight of his fellow Germans and to the poetic language of Hölderlin, is his attunement to the task of thinking as distinct from that of poetizing and in considering the difference between the two. Heidegger deems such an approach necessary if we are to initiate "an other building" (*ein anderes Bauen*) (GA 7: 195). This "other building" is, for Heidegger, only possible if we can attune ourselves to the dimension of dwelling that Hölderlin names "poetic" – that is, a dwelling attuned to the departure of the gods (what Heidegger terms "the abandonment of being") and to the human need to take measure of our contemporary god-forsakenness so as to allow for "an other dwelling." To think this other kind of dwelling as poetic, however, involves us in a fundamental reorientation to how we think about language.

There reigns in our contemporary relation to language the strange, yet prevalent, conviction that language is a tool by which and through which we communicate information. Heidegger understands this to be one of the inevitable results of *Gestell* that humans set upon language and attempt to gain mastery over it for the purpose of domination and dominion. At the beginning of the essay, much as he did at the outset of "Building Dwelling Thinking," Heidegger writes: "The human being acts as if *he* were the moulder and master of language, whereas, on the contrary, it is *language* that remains the master of the human being" (GA 7: 193, 148). If earlier Heidegger had emphasized that this failure on the part of humans to accept their humbler stature had driven them into a sense of unhomeliness, here Heidegger notes that "the human deteriorates into strange machinations." Only when we hear the appeal (*Zuspruch*) of language (*Sprache*) and correspond to it (*entsprechen*) can we authentically hear language's proper sound. For Heidegger, this happens authentically in the way poetry sounds its call. As early as his 1936 Rome lecture "Hölderlin and the Essence of Poetry," Heidegger made clear that language is not a ready-made tool lying around that poetry subsequently takes up and deploys. Rather, "poetry itself first makes language possible. . . . Thus, the essence of language must be understood out of the essence of poetry and not the other way around" (GA 4: 43/EHP: 60). ". . . poetically dwells the human being . . ." attempts to awaken its listeners to this singular call of language to hear what the poet says when he speaks of poetic dwelling.

Here Heidegger takes up again a theme from his first lecture course on Hölderlin's "Germania" – the exposure of the human being in the midst of beings, the one who "stands bareheaded beneath god's thunderstorms" (GA 39: 141; GA 7: 195; DKV I: 240). It appears, Heidegger tells us, as if in dwelling poetically "on this earth" that the human being is "torn away" from the earth (in the sense of *wegreissen*), exposed to the sky, and placed in the precarious position of being kept apart from it. But Heidegger replies that nothing could be farther from the truth – "Poetizing first brings the human onto the earth, unto it, and in this way brings it into dwelling" (GA 7: 196). But are we dwelling poetically in our shared time here upon the earth? And if not, why? Heidegger addresses these questions in a new way in this essay, a path that places a different emphasis on what we need to properly dwell. In "Building Dwelling Thinking" (1951) and "The Thing" (1949), Heidegger emphasized the fourfold and how our task is to protect (*schonen*), to preserve (*verwahren*), and to care for things in a way that lets them be as the things they are. In this way, by attending to things properly, we can build. Here, however, Heidegger does not employ the lexicon of protection, preservation, thinging, the fourfold, mirror-play, or Hölderlin's discourse about "das Rettende" (the saving). Instead, he comes to focus his efforts on unfolding the manifold senses of Hölderlin's word from "In lovely blueness . . .": measure (*Mass*). And yet despite this heavy emphasis on the question of measure, it would be a mistake to think that the fourfold does not play a significant role in this essay or that Heidegger has somehow left behind the human task of preservation and protection of things. Poetic dwelling involves all of these ways of tending to, cultivating, preserving, and protecting. Taken together, they serve as the fundamental ways of coming into nearness with things and in that way of enabling our sojourning, abiding, staying in the world – our *ethos*.

In this essay, as in the others written in the postwar era, the reigning concern for Heidegger is to confront a situation where technology has so extended its dominion over human ways of being that it becomes virtually unrecognizable. Foremost among these concerns is how thinking itself has become so imbricated in the matters and modalities of technological arrangement that it has lost its power of standing outside the labyrinth of *Gestell*. In his lectures of WS 1951–1952, "What Calls For(th) Thinking?," Heidegger goes so far as to argue that "it remains strange (*befremdlich*) and appears arrogant (*anmassend*) to maintain that the most thought-provoking in our precarious time is that we are still not yet thinking" (GA 8: 7–8). As Heidegger so famously put it, "science does not think." More than this, Heidegger strives to show how technology actively undermines all attempts at thinking. In an age where philosophy has given itself over to metaphysics and has become inured to a poetic form of thinking, Heidegger attempts to make us aware of the impoverishment of our current ways of thinking about thinking. To address this plight, Heidegger turns to Hölderlin in what he calls a "leap into thinking," a poetic thinking attuned to the dangers and precariousness of our current situation, yet also able to offer a different pathway into the kind of thinking needed in this age. Heidegger finds the impulse for such a leap in Hölderlin's word ". . . poetically dwells the human being" that poetizes measure as the unifying bond between thing and world, even as it gestures toward the divinities as a way to measure the human. To think this poetic measure in a way that does not fall into the traditional forms of conceptual representation or correspondence theory, Heidegger thinks measure in terms of absence and withdrawal rather than as a firm and enduring standard (*Mass-stab*). The thinking that thinks such a poetic measure can only think to the extent that such thinking lets itself be claimed by poetic measure rather than asserting it. Such a measure cannot be measured according to our usual standards of measurement. Rather, what the experience of poetic measure entails – as thinking – is a certain lack of measure, an incommensurable measure. The Latin word *mensura* has to do with "measure" and "measurement." It has etymological ties to words having to do with "table" (*mensa*), "month" (*mensis*), "menstruate" (*menstruare*), "semester" (*sex* + *mensis*), "immense" (*immensus*), and "dimension" (*dis* + *metiri*, "to measure off").[58] Yet what Heidegger finds in this word involves less the sense of mathematical measure than the rhythm, cadence, beat, or metric of a poetic line that provides the *Schwung* or impetus for the oscillation (*schwingen*) of a leap into thinking. It is language or, more precisely, poetic language that provides the *Schwung* to help us get on our way to thinking a poetic measure. In "The Western Conversation," the opening line of the text refers to the multiple senses of *Schwung* and *Schwingen* that Heidegger finds in Hölderlin's hymn "The Ister," around which the conversation revolves. *Schwung* here can be thought of as a vaulting leap or soaring that initiates a critical movement. In "The Ister," Hölderlin writes about the journey across the Ister from bank to bank and how it requires the vaulting momentum of wings:

> Not without wings (*Schwingen*) may someone
> Grasp for what is near . . .
> And reach the other side (*Und kommen auf die andere Seite*). (DKV I: 362)

Hölderlin's Ister hymn serves as a kind of *Wortschatz* (literally a "word-treasure" rather than mere vocabulary). There the poet offers words whose influence will resonate in the later works of Heidegger, words such as *das Schickliche* (the fitting) v. 10, *bauen* (building) v. 15, *wohnen* (dwelling) v. 22, *Mass* (measure) v. 25, among others. It is in conversation with this poetic lexicon that Heidegger seeks a passageway to an other kind of building and an other kind of dwelling. In "The Western Conversation," the Older Man comes to speak of "clearing the house of our dwelling" as he comes to the realization that "hearing the stirrings of poetic song" demands "the vaulting momentum of the eagle's wings (*der Schwung der Adlerschwingen*)" that deeply

---

[58] Michiel de Vaan, *Etymological Dictionary of Latin and Other Italic Languages* (Leiden: Brill, 2016), 372–373.

pervades our being" (GA 75: 87). Later on in the conversation, still grappling with the enigmatic language of the poem, the Older Man asks whether, in attuning ourselves to Hölderlin's poetic language, we will "be able to prepare the feast and found (*stiften*) the dwelling of the human being" (GA 75: 137). As part of this preparation, he poses the question: "Is it time to prepare the bridal feast on the other side [of the Ister] and thereby prepare the people of this land to dwell poetically on the other side?" (GA 75: 136) This is the question of dwelling that Heidegger will pose again in ". . . poetically dwells the human being" as he situates poetic dwelling and/as poetic thinking in relation to the possibility of dwelling "on the other side" in an other beginning.

4.3.2 Sojourn and Measure

Before he sets out on his discussion of poetic measure as a way to situate us beneath the sky and upon the earth, Heidegger cites some lines from "In lovely blueness":

> May, when life is all hardship, may a man look up and say: I too would like to resemble thee? Yes. As long as kindliness, which is pure, remains in his heart not unhappily a man may measure (*misset*) himself with the divinity. Is God unknown? Is he manifest (*offenbar*) as the sky? This rather I believe. Of the human, measure it is. Full with what is our due, yet poetically, dwells the human on this earth (*Voll Verdienst, doch dichterisch, wohnet der Mensch auf dieser Erde*).[59]

For Hölderlin, the measure of the human can never simply rest in the divine as a transcendent source of value. Nor can it be found upon the earth as that which grounds the measure in a familiar residence. Measure can neither be sequestered *diesseits oder jenseits*; that is, it cannot be located on earth as a temporal metronome or in the heavens as an eternal one. The relation between heaven and earth is as difficult as that between gods and humans. In this poem, Hölderlin attempts to introduce the sculptural image of Renaissance art – the *imago dei* (the human as the image of the divine) – and yet, for him, there remains an irreparable cleavage between the frailty of the human form and the deathless remove of the gods. Nonetheless, Hölderlin finds in this image of the incommensurability of the human and the divine a trace of a deeper union. For as he puts it, it is precisely in the absence of the gods (*deus absconditus*) that their presence makes itself manifest. As Heidegger comes to reflect on the possibility of poetic dwelling in an epoch of destitution and divine withdrawal, he finds in this poem a way to think a poetic measure that will serve as an

---

[59] Friedrich Hölderlin, DKV I: 479/*Poems and Fragments*, trans. Michael Hamburger (London: Anvil Press, 2004), 788–789 tm.

enigmatic and mysterious path into the fourfold unity of gods, mortals, earth, and sky. As Heidegger thinks it, poetic measure takes the measure of that which cannot be taken measure of. In others words it offers a *mensura* for what is incommensurable – the absence, withdrawal, and withholding of measure itself. Such a measure resides neither in the earth nor upon it; that is, it cannot be grounded in the human. It traverses, rather, the span of the human's dwelling between earth and sky.

Heidegger calls this realm of the between the "dimension" (in German: *Dimension*, from the Latin *mensura*, "measure"). As Heidegger puts it, the human glance upward toward the heavens "measures out (*durchmisst*) the between of sky and earth. This between is meted out to (*zugemessen*) the dwelling of the human. We now call the measuring out that is so apportioned, that is so reached, the dimension" (GA 7: 198/PLT: 220 tm). Heidegger then tells his listeners that he prefers to leave this dimension without bestowing upon it a name.

> The essence of the dimension is the meting out of the between that is cleared and thus spanned: of the upward reach to the sky as well as the downward reach to earth. . . .
>
> According to Hölderlin's words, the human measures out the dimension by measuring itself against the heavenly. The human does not undertake measuring out (*Durchmessen*) at some time or other. Rather, the human is first of all human only in such measuring out. That is why it can indeed try to obstruct, diminish, or disfigure such measuring out, but it can never elude it.
> (GA 7: 199/PLT 220–221 tm)

For Heidegger, the human being becomes commensurate with the measure of its reaching toward the sky when it accedes to the limit of such measuring. It is the dimension that metes out the between, not the human. The dimension offers an interstice of relations that encompasses the human's reach to the sky while setting a limit to such reach. This apportioning dimension of measure has long and distinguished roots in ancient Greek poetry and philosophy, going back to Pindar and Heraclitus.

In Fragments 30, 31, and 94, Heraclitus speaks to the power of measure as a cosmic force whose limits even the sun god Helios can never overstep. Moreover, Heraclitus tells us that *physis* has no beginning and no end, nor is it the product of human or divine *poiesis*. It is, rather, "an ever-flaming fire, flaring up according to measure and extinguishing according to measure."[60] For Pindar as well, we see the goddess Nemesis with her "stern scales" (Pythian Ode, X, v. 44) offering a limit to the excesses and transgressions of humans who

---

[60] Heidegger cites this Fragment in GA 29/30: 47. I cite here the translation from William McNeill & Nicholas Walker, *Fundamental Concepts of Metaphysics* (Bloomington: Indiana University Press, 1995), 31.

undertake their designs without an eye toward measure. In his Second Pythian Ode, Pindar offers this *gnome*:

> ... It is ever right to mark
> the measure (*metron*) of all things in the limits
> of one's own station.[61]

If, in the pietist discourse of Hölderlin's eighteenth-century world, this Pindaric measure would be treated as a moral precept stressing the dangers of unrestrained hybris (*Anmassung*) and excess (*Übermass*), the poet read this differently. What Pindar offered, he believed, was a poetic measure to structure the architectonic of the poem, a measure that fit the age in which the gods had absconded. Heidegger would, of course, follow this nonmoral reading of measure and come to think of it in terms of a poetic dwelling in the age of the world's night.

For Heidegger, the measure is never simply "there," present for us as a standard by which to gauge our direction or orient our journey. On the contrary, the proper measure is always already unknown and it is as this unknown that measure unfolds its most elemental power. Yet the poetic measure is one that demands of us a different kind of measuring, one attuned to concealment in a way that fosters the virtues of reticence, awe, reverence, and sparing. Such concealment demands a poetizing that lets things appear in their non-presence, and lets them be sheltered in a poetic idiom that refuses to adapt itself to a calculus of equivalence and availability. It is this poetics of the fourfold that situates dwelling in the nearness of the interface between things and world. As Andrew Mitchell so incisively puts it, "scientific measurement contains the measured; poetic measurement releases it."[62] Such a measure can find residence in neither earth nor sky, in neither the mortal nor the divine realm; it traverses, rather, the span of the human being's dwelling between earth and sky. Heidegger finds the expression of such a measure in the way Hölderlin poetizes the difficulty of finding such a measure. "In lovely blueness" addresses the frailty of any such hopes for securing a measure of/for/from the human:

> Is there a measure on earth? There is
> None/ Gibt es auf Erden ein Maas? Es gibt
> keines.[63]

---

[61] Pindar, *Olympian Odes, Pythian Odes*, trans. William Race (Cambridge: Harvard University Press, 1997), 234–235 tm. For a penetrating account of Pindar on measure, cf. Michael Theunissen, *Pindar: Menschenlos und Wende der Zeit* (Munich: Beck, 2000), 808–815 & 847–860.

[62] Andrew Mitchell, *The Fourfold*, 125.

[63] Friedrich Hölderlin, DKV I: 479/*Poems and Fragments*, 788–789 tm.

In his carefully drawn language, Hölderlin sets up an oppositional structure that juxtaposes the height of a church steeple with the movement of swallows, the sounding of a weathercock, and the trees of the wood. Natural sounds, rhythms, and movement will get set in tension with the human-made sounds of a bell tower and the descent from the tower's steps. The blueness of the sky contrasts with the lovely blueness that "blossoms" in the steeple's metal roof. With all of this careful detail, Hölderlin reflects upon the Heraclitean law of opposites wherein all things that come to be do so only in and through opposition. What Heidegger draws from his reading of the poem is nothing less than a fundamental insight into an understanding of poetic measure. To put this in Heideggerian terms: Measure does not inhere in beings; it can only emerge in their distinction from being. Measure is a relation, a movement, an event, rather than a stationary standard whose status lies in standing presence. Heidegger finds such a relation in Hölderlin's way of approaching god: "God is unknown for Hölderlin and it is precisely as this Unknown One that he is the measure for the poet" (GA 7: 201/PLT: 222 tm). Heidegger then adds:

> What is the measure for human measuring? God? No! The sky? No! The manifestness of the sky? No! The measure consists in the way in which the god who remains unknown, is revealed as the unknown through the sky. The appearance of the god through the sky consists in an unveiling that lets what conceals itself be seen, but not in such a way that seeks to rend what is concealed from its concealment. Rather, the letting be seen happens only through a safeguarding of the concealed in its self-concealment. In this way the unknown god appears as the unknown through the manifestness of the sky. This appearance is the measure (*Mass*), by which the human measures itself (*sich misset*). (GA 7: 201/PLT: 223 tm)

By expressing the power of concealment as a poetic force that bears witness to the difficult and fragile measuring of the human being in its relation to that which exceeds it, Heidegger manages to think the incommensurability of Hölderlin's *deus absconditus* and the displacement of human dwelling. Heidegger terms this "a strange measure," one that unsettles us in both a metaphorical and literal sense since it is "ungewöhnlich" – inhabitual, non-customary, but, more strictly, lacking consonance with our dwelling place or *Wohnung*. Hölderlin had always understood this displacement as part of our human identity. For him, the human is the one who is foreign to itself, alien to its home, always estranged in a strange, unsettling way from its own settlements. In his work, poetry takes the measure of such estrangement, seeing in the figures of Greek tragedy such as Oedipus and Antigone the deepest expression of our bifurcated, chiastic identity. In the radical disjunction of Oedipus' insight and blindness, in Antigone's oxymoronic "crime of piety," Hölderlin finds less the human made in the image of god (*imago dei*) than a being beset by its own deficits, lacking a center, adrift and destitute, a stranger to the world, but even more a stranger to itself. And yet this poetic measure of the human is not one of mere alienation or anomie that could be ameliorated through social engineering. On the contrary, Hölderlin finds in such estrangement an essential element in helping the human being to find its proper dwelling place upon the earth, one that would consist in attending to our homelessness and estranged being as what intimately belongs to the promise of homecoming. Homecoming here is understood, quite naturally, as a homecoming to what is one's own, what is native and proper to one. At the same time, however, Hölderlin poetizes a strange and other form of homecoming – what we might think of as an "alien homecoming" since at the heart of what is one's own lies precisely something unhomely, *ungewöhnlich*, strange, and alien. Heidegger captures something of this alien and uncanny aspect of Hölderlin's poetic task at the end of his ". . . poetically dwells the human" essay where he cites Hölderlin's short poem "What is God?"

> What is God? unknown, yet
> Full of qualities is the face
> Of heaven with him. For lightning flashes
> And wrath are a god's. The more a thing
> Is invisible, it sends itself into the foreign . . .
> (*Jemehr ist eins/unsichtbar, schicket es sich in Fremdes*). (GA 7: 203–204)[64]

Like the sudden shock of lightning flashes and thunder, god's way of revealing is marked by strangeness and alterity. In Hölderlin's poetic theophany, the gods appear as strange and foreign, their presence marked by absence and recission. It is in taking the measure of such absence and recission that the poet can hope to offer a poetic measure of "the darkness and silence of what is alien" (GA 7: 205).

Yet Heidegger reminds us that what is alien to god is what is familiar to the human being: "In that which is familiar to the human, but strange to god, the unknown sends itself in order to remain there protected as the unknown" (GA 7: 204). Dwelling can only take place authentically when it receives this poetic insight into the relation of the familiar and the alien, when it *lets* sky be sky as what is not the earth but is nonetheless bound to earth as its other, as what allows earth to flourish under its lovely blueness. Moreover, Heidegger will find in this poetic gesture of letting a way to challenge Oedipus' own tragic insistence on

---

[64] See also Friedrich Hölderlin, DKV I: 384/*Poems and Fragments:* 614–615. An alternate translation of the last two lines of "What is God?" might read: "The more something/ is unseen, it goes forth into what is alien" (or even: "It dispenses itself in strange ways").

control, dominion, interdiction, and excessive scrutiny. At the end of "In lovely blueness," Hölderlin highlights these unmeasured characteristics of Oedipus and writes: "King Oedipus has one eye too many, perhaps."[65] In his "Notes on Oedipus," Hölderlin remarks that we find in Oedipus "a knowledge that has torn through its limits, as if intoxicated in its own majestical, harmonious form," leading him to a "a wrathful immoderation" (DKV II: 852). For Heidegger, then, Oedipus comes to stand for the kind of frantic excess of an age driven by its own machinational drive for dominion over the earth, an age that has lost any sense of a proper measure for dwelling. Heidegger's essay offers a quite different path for human residence, one marked by an *ethos* committed to the sense that "poetizing and dwelling belong together, each reciprocally requiring the other, together" (GA 7: 206/PLT: 227 tm). Yet the promise of poetic dwelling is hardly one that can come to pass without a sense of releasement to that which is coming, what Hölderlin understands as a proper preparation for the coming of the gods. Without putting forward an ethics for such an expectation, Heidegger keeps to his task of showing how we require an *ethos* of poetic dwelling if we are to ever fulfill the promise of "an other building." The task of the thinker in such an epoch is, like that of the poet, to think the poetic measure of our dwelling according to a "diminished measure" (*verringerten Mass-stab*) (DKV II: 920). That is, to stand back from our Oedipal filiation with command, control, and dominion and let the enigma of being be released into its own way of appearance. The later Heidegger terms this kind of *ethos* "Gelassenheit," a releasement to things, a comportment of letting being prevail as letting-be – not a passive acceptance of things or an active attempt to direct such releasement. As Ian Moore has suggested in his thoughtful book, *Eckhart, Heidegger, and The Imperative of Releasement*, "The doing that is proper to *Gelassenheit* involves and demands both a letting-be and being-let, a preparation and a being prepared."[66] Poetic dwelling, like poetic thinking, demands such letting as well. If sometimes Heidegger's own human, all too human emphasis on a singular form of German exceptionalism mars these efforts at a genuinely poetic thinking of the foreign, the alien, and the uncanny, we should not lose sight of the fact that Heidegger's thinking, as a poetic thinking, has no room for such an embrace of the German *Sonderweg*. And yet as we have seen throughout this Element, Heidegger's work comes to us laden with its own attachments to an ideal of German exceptionalism that threatens such poetic thinking at its core. Any attempt to think along with Heidegger on this path of poetic thinking needs to be

---

[65] Friedrich Hölderlin, DKV II: 852/*Poems and Fragments*: 790–791.
[66] Ian Alexander Moore, *Eckhart, Heidegger, and the Imperative of Releasement* (Albany: State University of New York Press, 2019).

aware of the byways and detours in the thickets of such exceptionalism that imperil his whole project.

Concluding ...

To have lost our measure of dwelling means nothing less than to have lost our connection to the earth. It means to have become homeless. Heidegger returns to this fundamental topos again and again. In the "Letter on Humanism," he remarks: "Homelessness is coming to be the destiny of the world" (GA 9: 339/PM: 258). In "Sprache und Heimat," he writes: "The human is homeless" (GA 13: 157). In *Four Seminars*, he asks: "Is there now, in these times, still something like an 'at home', a dwelling, an abode? No, there are 'dwelling machines,' urban clusters, in short: an industrialized product, but no longer a *home*" (GA 15: 389/FS: 74). What strikes Heidegger as the most egregious (and paradoxical) facet of this lack (loss) of home is that we have now come to be at home in our homelessness – but in a way radically different than the homelessness we earlier identified with Antigone. For Heidegger, Antigone's greatness lies in her "becoming homely in being unhomely" in such a way that she expresses the tragic depth of genuine poetic dwelling: In embracing her uncanny existence, she reveals how "the human potential for being, in its relation to being, is poetic" (GA 53: 150–151/HI: 120–121). Moreover, Heidegger will attest that "the unhomely being homely of human beings upon the earth is 'poetic'." Yet in our own sojourn upon the earth, beneath the sky, we become enmeshed in the implacable destining of *Gestell* to the extent that we become oblivious to our situation and even when we do address it, we fall back upon timeworn human strategies for ameliorating it. Yet Heidegger reminds us of the Hölderlinian logic of an alien homecoming by which any genuine stay in the homeland depends upon a sojourn into the foreign. And here the fate of Antigone provides us with the grammar for an *ethos* of poetic dwelling. By embracing the abyssal *Ab-grund* at the heart of being, Antigone embraces the alterity that consti- tutes the heart of Sophoclean tragedy. For Heidegger, this means that to find our own way home, we need to let go of our own strategies of management, arrange- ment, and presumptuousness (*Anmassung*), embodied in Creon, and let Antigone by our guide. Antigone, Heidegger tells us, "is the purest poem," her way of receiving the uncanny, the unhomely, the foreignness of beyng's way of manifest- ing, places her in nearness to "what is fitting" (*das Schickliche*). In her own fateful way, she offers a poetic measure to contrast with Creon's technological imperative to rule and dominate. It is Antigone's supreme accomplishment, on Heidegger's reading, that she gives herself over to being and releases herself from the quotidian demands of the human being. And here, I would argue, we find the pulse of Heidegger's poetic thinking, a thinking attuned to the foreign, the unhomely, the abyssal; a thinking that finds the proper measure of the human being in its openness to the possibility of poetic dwelling. But what else would poetic dwelling be than a thinking relation to all that is, than a way of dwelling, attuned to the mirror-play of the fourfold, that safeguards and protects the earth?

During the 1950s, Heidegger delivered a series of talks in small villages and towns in Southern Germany and Switzerland that addressed the question of dwelling, addresses that had at their center the themes of *Heimat, Sprache, Dichtung*, and *Denken*.[67] Perhaps the most famous of these *Heimatreden* was the 1955 address he delivered in his hometown of Messkirch, commemorating the 175th anniversary of the composer Conradin Kreutzer. The citizens had gathered that day in Messkirch to celebrate what they termed a *Gedenkfeier*, understood usually as a "commemoration" of the dead. Yet Heidegger took his fellow townspeople at their word and offered his own form of a *Gedenkfeier*, which he took to mean a feast of commemorative thinking. The theme that sounds through-out this short piece is a simple one: "the contemporary human is in flight from thinking" (GA 16: 519). This flight is marked by a thorough-going "thoughtless-ness" which grows more perilous since humans will not acknowledge this pervasive state of impoverishment in their thinking. And yet Heidegger empha-sizes that "the human being, in the ground of its essence, has the capability to think" and, moreover, has as its vocation "thinking." Heidegger goes further here to acknowledge that "many Germans have lost their homeland" and that this "loss of rootedness" can be traced back to "the spirit of the age in which we were all born" (GA 16: 522). He then goes on to address the question of the deployment of a new form of calculative thinking that he ties to "the power concealed in modern technology" and acknowledges two different kinds of uncanniness (*Unheimlichkeit*). The first kind of uncanny/*unheimlich* change is that the world is becoming wholly technical: hydrogen bombs, atomic energy, and spaceships are being developed; we are also witnessing the technical transformation in agriculture, in urban patterns of dwelling, as well as in new modes of commercial transport. The second kind of uncanniness Heidegger notices is one whereby we remain unprepared for this transformation, with an inability to confront what is transpiring in our epoch. To address this form of uncanniness, Heidegger pro-poses a thinking that he terms "meditative thinking" (*besinnliches Denken*). This meditative thinking involves a letting-go of the demand for technological control in those relations to things not driven by the model of production, management, and delivery. And as he outlines the virtues of this meditative thinking, he urges his listeners: "let us give it a try."

---

[67] Most of these are collected in GA 13, *Aus der Erfahrung des Denkens*. "Gelassenheit" appears in GA 16: 517–529.

As part of his attempt to show his audience how to initiate this "releasement toward things" (*Gelassenheit zu den Dingen*), Heidegger cites the famous *Heimatdichter*, Johann Peter Hebel. And though Heidegger doesn't develop a strong connection to poetic thinking in his lecture, the groundwork is prepared for an understanding of how poetic language shows a deep affinity for releasement, meditative thinking, and the language of sojourn, stay, and dwelling. It is within such thinking that Heidegger suggests that we might find a pathway out of the cybernetic thinking that threatens the earth with the loss of homeland. Heidegger develops this connection in another lecture from 1956, "Hebel, Friend of the House." There Heidegger once again shows how it is in the language of the homeland (*Heimatsprache*) that we find a way to address the effects of the *Gestell* that have turned language into an instrument for calculative thinking and/ as machination. In this Hebel essay, Heidegger contrasts the attuned mode of poetic saying to what he terms "the language machine" (*Sprachmaschine*), which he distinguishes sharply from *die Sprechmaschine* (the speaking machine). The *Sprechmaschine* is an apparatus that records and reproduces speech – a tape recorder, a dictaphone, or any version of a sound-recording device. In the modern forms of voice recognition software, AI-generated translation programs, or the data-recorder, Heidegger's vision of modern instrumental language programming has come to realization. All of these new forms of the speaking machine betray, however, an ever deeper affinity with a new machinational relation to language whereby all language becomes automatically subsumed under the aegis of the language machine. With all of these new technological devices, "the impression is still maintained that the human masters the *Sprachmaschine*. In truth, however, it may be that the *Sprachmaschine* sets language into an operation and in this way masters the essence of the human" (GA 13: 149). With the onset of such a process, language becomes another essential component in service to the instrumentality of *Gestell*, one that separates our authentic dwelling place – language – from the promise of poetic dwelling upon the earth. In conjunction with this insight into the fragmentation and loss of an originary relation to language, Heidegger attempts to rethink our own relation to the earth. As Kelly Oliver has persuasively argued, Heidegger's talk of earth in the late work on the fourfold cannot merely be understood as a "nostalgic longing for some fantasy of home as presence." It is, rather, she argues, an earnest attempt "to avoid the totalizing and homogenizing universalism of globalism," one that formulates "an ethics of the earth" as an antidote to global-planetary thinking.[68]

---

[68] Kelly Oliver, *Earth and World: Philosophy after the Apollo Mission* (New York: Columbia University Press, 2015), 113–114.

Part of what I have been attempting to emphasize in this Cambridge Element is how Heidegger's poetic thinking has a crucial role to play in offering a counterbalance to the kind of global-planetary (non)-thinking that has gripped our epoch. In his earliest reflections, Heidegger had already noted that "poetizing is the sustaining ground of history" (GA 4: 43). More than this, however, Heidegger had insisted that "poetizing is the founding naming of being and of the essence of all things." Moreover, he would claim that "human existence is poetic in its ground." As part of this selfsame designation of poetizing, Heidegger stressed that "poetizing itself first makes language possible" since "the essence of language must be understood out of the essence of poetizing and not the other way around." Corollary to such a vision of the poetic, of course, is the towering role of Hölderlin in Heidegger's poetic thinking, since it is Hölderlin who "thinks beyond into the ground and middle of being" (GA 4: 47). In concert with Hölderlin, as a way to think otherwise than through the metaphysical conceptuality of both the scientific and the philosophical traditions, Heidegger turns to the thematics of poetic dwelling as a way to counter the epochal "danger" (*Gefahr*) of *Gestell*. Here with Hölderlin's own poetic language as his companion, Heidegger attempts to prepare the path of a different kind of thinking, a poetic thinking attuned to the *poiesis* of *Hervorbringen*, of "letting what presences come forth into appearance" (GA 7: 28). This kind of *poiesis*, as Will McNeill reminds us, "brings into being the *poiesis* of world itself."[69] As he puts it, "In first letting a world appear and come into being, poetizing in its essence originarily configures the dwelling site of human beings, their *ethos*." What differentiates the mere composing of poetic works (in the sense of poesy) from poetizing is precisely this poietic dimension of letting a world appear and of configuring a site of dwelling for human beings. To think of poetizing as an *ethos* means understanding language as something other than a human possession. It means attuning ourselves to a different sense of both poetizing and thinking, one whereby we come to experience language less as a tool or as an instrument for communication than as "the clearing-concealing advent of being itself" (GA 9: 326).

As the author of some of the most insightful writing on Heidegger and language, Krzysztof Ziarek has emphasized how poetizing prepares a path for meditative thinking, one that lies beyond philosophy. By reenergizing language and helping it move out of its usual province of making statements or setting up systems of signs, "*Dichten* marks the possible pivot which may give direction to the preparatory thinking envisioned by Heidegger."[70] Such poetic thinking is not

---

[69] William McNeill, *The Time of Life: Heidegger and 'Ethos*, 143.

[70] Krzysztof Ziarek, "The Event's Foreign Vernacular: *Denken* and *Dichten* in Heidegger," in Andrew Benjamin, ed., *Heidegger and Literature* (Cambridge: Cambridge University Press, 2023), 44–45. I want to thank Professor Ziarek for making this available to me before publication.

goal-oriented; it opens up a path of movement, a being on-the-way that situates us in our sojourn upon the earth, one that constitutes our dwelling. But dwelling should not be understood as a place of fixity or settlement. Rather, as we saw in Heidegger's reading of *Antigone* and the Ister, poetic dwelling is essentially not of the home; it is, rather, *unheimlich*. In dwelling in such an unhomely way, we thereby expose ourselves to the very movement and momentum of our temporal moment, bound up as it is with "the event of an originary *poiesis* of which we are not the origin, yet which, happening in and through us, first enables our dwelling."[71] One of the uncanny aspects of the Ister lectures is the way they show how "dwelling itself, being homely, is the becoming homely of a being unhomely" (GA 53: 171). Moreover, through their focus on the homely, they express, almost literally, how the river's "home" is its movement toward, through, and away from its home. This is why Heidegger can say at the end of his lecture course that "The poet is the river. And the river is the poet" (GA 53: 203–204/HI: 165–167). Both the poet and the river "poetically ground the dwelling of humans upon this earth." Heidegger ends his course by emphasizing how "This poetry demands of us a transformation in our ways of thinking and experiencing, one that concerns being in its entirety." And his last word makes allusion to Hölderlin's second letter to Böhlendorff, where the poet writes that his experiences in Bordeaux and on his journey home to Nürtingen, exposed him to "the violent element, the fire of heaven" (DKV III: 466). This took hold of the poet so deeply that Hölderlin tells his friend that it is as if "Apollo has struck me." At the end of the Ister lectures, Heidegger returns to this selfsame experience of the poet's exposure to the fire of the sun and to Apollo's force, enjoining his listeners to "let go" of our "allegedly actual" understanding of what rivers "are," and of what poets presumable "are" "so as to enter that free realm in which the poetic is." Only if we let go of our customary standards and gauges of measure and acknowledge, like Hölderlin, that there is no present, available measure on earth might we enter that place where we can experience what has been poetized and from whence such poetizing has its origin. Only then, Heidegger admonishes, can we hope to enter into the originary force of poetic thinking: "Yet if we are strong enough to think, then it may be sufficient for us to ponder merely from afar – that is, scarcely – the truth of this poetry and what it poetizes, so that we may suddenly be struck by it" (GA 53: 2–5/HI: 167).

Entering into the realm of poetic thinking, Heidegger wants to say, demands being open to the suddenness of the moment; it requires a willingness to being exposed to Apollo's fire. There is certainly risk involved here. Being exposed to fire from heaven, to "the violent element" (*das gewaltige Element*), involves for

---

[71] William McNeill, *The Time of Life: Heidegger and 'Ethos,* xvii.

Hölderlin an exposure to what is *deinon*. In his Ister lectures, Heidegger names this "the fundamental word of Greek antiquity" (GA 53: 82/HI:67). In his own translation of *Antigone*, Hölderlin renders it as *ungeheuer* – inhabitual, out of the ordinary, frightful, monstrous (DKV II: 873). Yet Heidegger will translate *deinon* as *unheimlich* – uncanny, awesome, aw(e)ful, that which is not of the home. But Sophocles also employs the word *deinon* to describe the plight of Oedipus and he links this to Oedipus' outburst at the end of the play where he blames Apollo for bringing his sorrows to completion. It is at that precise moment in the drama that the chorus identifies Oedipus as "the doer of dreadful (*deina*) deeds" (v. 1327).[72] Hölderlin will translate this into German as *gewaltiges* and will think it, as in his second Böhlendorff letter, as what binds him to Apollo. In terms of our reading of Heidegger's Ister lectures and, in a larger sense, of his understanding of poetic thinking, what matters here is how such thinking exposes us to the doubling ambiguities of Apollo's realm of fire – its creative as well as destructive elements. Being struck by Apollo's fire means risking the kind of immolation experienced by Empedocles, the poet-philosopher "going down in holy flames," the one to whom in Hölderlin's tragedy *The Death of Empedocles*, Pausanius charges:

> You wish to be someone other than the one you are,
> Insufficient to your honor, you give yourself over
> To that which is alien. (DKV II: 379)

Empedocles himself recognizes his own uncanny, liminal status as the one caught between the demand to be authentically at home in who he is and yet open to the alien. He will later tell Pausanius in forthright terms: "I am not who I am" (DKV II: 406). For Heidegger, as for Hölderlin, to be a poet-philosopher involves being at risk, being attuned to the uncanny, *unheimlich*, *ungeheuer*, violent, and inhabitual forces that shape our dwelling. Empedocles is hardly any arbitrary figure for Heidegger. In his earliest set of Hölderlin lectures from WS 1934/35, Heidegger cites a long passage from *The Death of Empedocles* that refers to Antigone, a passage he will later cite in the Ister lectures (GA 39: 215–216; GA 53: 70). There he will forge the connection between Empedocles, Antigone, and what he calls "a founding (*Stiftung*) of the entire Greek Dasein," one that first enables human beings to settle on the earth. "This dwelling is grounded in and through poetizing," Heidegger emphasizes; it transports humans "into the realm of a threatening of beyng." For Hölderlin, it is in figures such as Empedocles, Antigone, and Oedipus that he finds that willingness and necessity to step outside of the ordinary and expose oneself to the uncanny doubleness of *physis*. Such

---

[72] Sophokles, *Dramen* (Munich: Artemis, 1985), 364.

uncanniness cannot be merely circumscribed in the realm of the human, the subjective, the psychological. Such unsettling lies at the heart of any attempt to challenge the measures imposed in our habitual haunts and habitats. In this sense, poetic dwelling, much as the poetic thinking that makes it possible, is less about settlement, residency, or the fixity of habitation than it is about opening to the power of the alien. It involves the risk that Hölderlin poetized at the end of his hymn "As on a holiday . . .," of the poet as a false priest who, like Empedocles (and Tantalus), risks the uncanny reversal of being blessed and then cursed by the gods. As Hölderlin wrote in his ode "Empedocles"

> You seek life, you search for it, and there wells and gleams
> A divine fire deep from the earth to you
> And shuddering with desire, you
> Hurl yourself down into Aetna's flames. (DKV I: 241)

Hölderlin's *Empedocles* drama affirms the human belonging to the earth, yet it also recognizes the danger of the alien element. To be able to enter the intimacy of a bond with the earth requires the risk of self-dissolution, as Empedocles knew all too well. To be able to enter into an intimacy with the homeland and with authentic poetic dwelling involves the risk of losing one's home. When Heidegger thinks this risk, he thinks it poetically in conversation with Hölderlin and Sophocles, specifically in terms of their poetizing of the unhomeliness of the human. To be at home for him always means exposing ourselves to what is not of the home, what is strange, alien, and other. Here Hölderlin's Empedocles stands with Oedipus and Antigone as those figures who risked the unhomeliness of being so as to find their home in being. It is well to remember this crucial element of the unhomely and the alien when considering Heidegger's thinking on homeland, dwelling, and homecoming. For Heidegger grasps the essential role of the alien/foreign in any thinking of the native, the national, and the proper. We see this foregrounded in the Ister lectures where the tropes of homeland, *Heimat* and poetic dwelling, are intimately bound to both language and the geographical course of the river. Rivers have to do with movement from source to mouth; they have to do with change, variation, and the rhythmic pulse of flow and counter-flow, much as the poetic language of "The Ister" itself. For Heidegger, Hölderlin's poetizing of the river offers not a description "of" the Ister; rather, such poetizing *is* the river itself. Both the poetizing and the river move back and forth between journey and return, *Ausflug* and *Rückkehr*, as well as between asylum and exile. Rivers tear apart the land, leaving them torn and riven. In this way, they fulfill the Hölderlinian law of homecoming and return that, as Heidegger puts it, "tears (*herausreisst*) human beings out of the habitual middle of their lives" (GA 53: 32). Only in this way, torn from out of the habitual (*gewöhnlich*), can the human being genuinely find a proper dwelling (*Wohnung*). Only in being attuned to the alien character of homecoming can the human being ever find a way to dwell poetically upon the earth. This chiastic insight into the counter-turning logic of alien homecoming as requiring a turn to the foreign lies at the heart of Heidegger's poetic thinking. It remains an essential part in any attempt to think the problem of dwelling, *Aufenthalt*, sojourn, and *ethos*. More than this, it shapes Heidegger's understanding of the site of human dwelling as one marked by exile and yet one which we all share in the time and place allotted to us.

In the wake of the last decade's unsettling revelations about Heidegger's political and racial pronouncements in the Black Notebooks, we cannot ignore his all too human departure from the insights of his own thinking. These revelations will always provide cause for concern about Heidegger's own errant path of political engagement. And yet it would be irresponsible of us were we to thereby reduce all of Heidegger's work to these singular pronouncements. What I have tried to argue here is that we can also find in this work an understanding of poetic thinking that offers a fertile alternative to the kind of technical, computational, algorithmic thinking that threatens to take over the very task of thinking otherwise. Heidegger's engagement with Hölderlin and with the poetic language of the German tradition puts forward an alternative path for addressing our own situation of thinking in an epoch of deficit, destitution, and default. It is precisely within such a situation that Heidegger's writings call upon us to reexamine the fundaments of our thinking and to heed the summons of a different kind of thinking, a poetic thinking whose time is not yet, but whose time is still to come.

Abbreviations

Note: Unless otherwise indicated, all translations from the German are my own.

SS   Spring Semester
WS   Winter Semester

Heidegger

BN   *Ponderings II-VI: Black Notebooks, 1931–1938.* Trans. Richard Rojcewicz. Bloomington: Indiana University Press, 2016.

BT   *Being and Time.* Trans. Dennis Schmidt. Albany: State University of New York Press, 2010.

BW   *Basic Writings.* Ed. David F. Krell. New York: Harper & Row, 1977.

CP   *Contributions to Philosophy.* Trans. Richard Rojcewicz & Daniela Vallega-Neu. Bloomington: Indiana University Press, 2012.

E   *The Event.* Trans. Richard Rojcewicz. Bloomington: Indiana University Press, 2013.

EHP   *Elucidations of Hölderlin's Poetry.* Trans. Keith Hoeller. New York: Humanity Books, 2000.

EM   *Einführung in die Metaphysik.* Tübingen: Niemeyer, 1953.

FS   *Four Seminars.* Trans. Andrew Mitchell and Francóis Raffoul. Bloomington: Indiana University Press, 2003.

G   *Gelassenheit.* Pfullingen: Neske, 1988.

GA   *Gesamtausgabe.* Frankfurt: Klostermann, 1975 ff.

GA 2   *Sein und Zeit.* Ed. Friedrich-Wilhelm von Herrmann. Frankfurt: Klostermann, 1977.

GA 4   *Erläuterungen zu Hölderlins Dichtung.* Ed. Friedrich-Wilhelm von Herrmann. Frankfurt: Klostermann, 1981.

GA 5   *Holzwege.* Ed. Friedrich-Wilhelm von Herrmann. Frankfurt: Klostermann, 1977.

GA 7   *Vorträge und Aufsätze.* Ed. Friedrich-Wilhelm von Herrmann. Frankfurt: Klostermann, 2000.

GA 8   *Was heisst Denken?* Ed. Paola-Ludovika Coriando. Frankfurt: Klostermann, 2002.

GA 9   *Wegmarken.* Ed. Friedrich-Wilhelm von Herrmann. Frankfurt: Klostermann, 2004.

GA 11   *Identität und Differenz.* Ed. Friedrich-Wilhelm von Herrmann. Frankfurt: Klostermann, 2006.

GA 12   *Unterwegs zur Sprache.* Ed. Friedrich-Wilhelm von Herrmann. Frankfurt: Klostermann, 1985.

GA 13   *Aus der Erfahrung des Denkens.* Ed. Hermann Heidegger. Frankfurt: Klostermann, 2002.

GA 14   *Zur Sache des Denkens.* Ed. Friedrich-Wilhelm von Herrmann. Frankfurt: Klostermann, 2007.

GA 15   *Seminare.* Ed. Curd Ochwadt. Frankfurt: Klostermann, 1986.

GA 16   *Reden und andere Zeugnisse eines Lebensweges.* Ed. Hermann Heidegger. Frankfurt: Klostermann, 2000.

GA 38   *Über Logik als die Frage nach dem Wesen der Sprache.* Ed. Günter Seubold. Frankfurt: Klostermann, 1998.

GA 39   *Hölderlins Hymne "Germanien" und "Der Rhein."* Ed. Susanne Ziegler. Frankfurt: Klostermann, 1989.

GA 40   *Einführung in die Metaphysik.* Ed. Petra Jaeger. Frankfurt: Klostermann, 1983.

GA 45   *Grundfragen der Philosophie.* Ed. Friedrich-Wilhelm von Herrmann. Frankfurt: Klostermann, 1992.

GA 50   *Nietzsches Metaphysik.* Ed. Petra Jaeger. Frankfurt: Klostermann, 1990.

GA 52   *Hölderlins Hymne "Andenken."* Ed. Curd Ochwadt. Frankfurt: Klostermann, 1992.

GA 53   *Hölderlins Hymne "Der Ister."* Ed. Walter Biemel. Frankfurt: Klostermann, 1993.

GA 54   *Parmenides.* WS 1942/43. Edited by Manfred S. Frings. Frankfurt: Klostermann, 1992.

GA 55   *Heraklit.* I. *Der Anfang des abendländischen Denkens*; II. *Logik. Heraklits Lehre des Logos.* Ed. Manfred S. Frings. Frankfurt: Klostermann, 1994.

GA 65   *Beiträge zur Philosophie.* Ed. Friedrich-Wilhelm von Herrmann. Frankfurt: Klostermann, 1989.

GA 66   *Besinnung.* Ed. Friedrich-Wilhelm von Herrmann. Frankfurt: Klostermann, 1997.

GA 69   *Die Geschichte des Seyns.* Ed. Peter Trawny. Frankfurt: Klostermann, 1998.

GA 70   *Über den Anfang.* Ed. Paola-Ludovika Coriando. Frankfurt: Klostermann, 2005.

GA 71   *Das Ereignis.* Ed. Friedrich-Wilhelm von Herrmann. Frankfurt: Klostermann, 2009.

GA 73   *Zum Ereignis-Denken.* Ed. Peter Trawny. Frankfurt: Klostermann, 2013.

GA 75   *Zu Hölderlin-Griechenlandreisen.* Ed. Curd Ochwadt. Frankfurt: Klostermann, 2000.

GA 80   *Vorträge.* Ed. Günther Neumann. Frankfurt: Klostermann, 2016-2020.

GA 81   *Gedachtes.* Ed. Paola-Ludovika Coriando. Frankfurt: Klostermann, 2007.

GA 94   *Überlegungen, II-VI (Schwarze Hefte, 1931–1938).* Ed. Peter Trawny. Frankfurt: Klostermann, 2014.

GA 95   *Überlegungen, VII-XI (Schwarze Hefte, (1938/1939).* Ed. Peter Trawny. Frankfurt: Klostermann, 2014.

GA 96   *Überlegungen, XII-XV (Schwarze Hefte, 1939–1941).* Ed. Peter Trawny. Frankfurt: Klostermann, 2014.

GA 97   *Anmerkungen I-V (Schwarze Hefte, 1942–1948).* Ed. Peter Trawny. Frankfurt: Klostermann, 2015.

GA 98   *Anmerkungen VI-IX (Schwarze Hefte, 1948/49–1951).* Ed. Peter Trawny. Frankfurt: Klostermann, 2018.

HGR   *Hölderlin's Hymns "Germania" and "The Rhine."* Trans. William McNeill and Julia Davis. Bloomington: Indiana University Press, 1996.

HI   *Hölderlin's Hymn "The Ister."* Trans. William McNeill and Julia Ireland. Bloomington: Indiana University Press, 2014.

IM   *Introduction to Metaphysics.* Trans. Gregory Fried and Richard Polt. New Haven: Yale University Press, 2014.

OBT   *Off the Beaten Track.* Trans. Julian Young and Kenneth Haynes. Cambridge University Press, 2002.

OWL   *On the Way to Language.* Trans. Peter Hertz. New York: Harper & Row, 1982.

P   *Parmenides.* Trans. Andre Schuwer and Richard Rojcewicz. Bloomington: Indiana University Press, 1992.

PLT   *Poetry, Language, Thought.* Trans. Albert Hofstadter. New York: Harper and Row, 1971.

PM   *Pathmarks.* Ed. William McNeill. Cambridge: Cambridge University Press, 1998.

Hölderlin

DKV   Deutscher Klassiker Verlag Ausgabe. Ed. Jochen Schmidt. In *Sämtliche Werke und Briefe in drei Bänden.* Frankfurt: Deutscher Klassiker Verlag, 2004.

ELT   *Hölderlin: Essays and Letters on Theory.* Ed. Thomas Pfau. Albany: State University of New York Press, 1988.

E&L   *Essays and Letters.* Ed. Jeremy Adler and Charlie Louth. Harmondsworth: Penguin, 2009.

SPF   *Selected Poems and Fragments.* Trans. Michael Hamburger. Harmondsworth: Penguin, 1998.

The Philosophy of Martin Heidegger

About the Editors

Filippo Casati

Lehigh University

Filippo Casati is an Assistant Professor at Lehigh University. He has published an array of articles in such venues as *The British Journal for the History of Philosophy, Synthese, Logic et Analyse, Philosophia, Philosophy Compass* and *The European Journal of Philosophy.* He is the author of *Heidegger and the Contradiction of Being* (Routledge) and, with Daniel O. Dahlstrom, he edited *Heidegger on logic* (Cambridge University Press).

Daniel O. Dahlstrom

Boston University

Daniel O. Dahlstrom, John R. Silber Professor of Philosophy at Boston University, has edited twenty volumes, translated Mendelssohn, Schiller, Hegel, Husserl, Heidegger, and Landmann-Kalischer, and authored Heidegger's *Concept of Truth* (2001), *The Heidegger Dictionary* (2013; second extensively expanded edition, 2023), *Identity, Authenticity, and Humility* (2017) and over 185 essays, principally on 18th-20th century German philosophy. With Filippo Casati, he edited *Heidegger on Logic* (Cambridge University Press).

About the Series

A continual source of inspiration and controversy, the work of Martin Heidegger challenges thinkers across traditions and has opened up previously unexplored dimensions of Western thinking. The Elements in this series critically examine the continuing impact and promise of a thinker who transformed early twentieth-century phenomenology, spawned existentialism, gave new life to hermeneutics, celebrated the truthfulness of art and poetry, uncovered the hidden meaning of language and being, warned of "forgetting" being, and exposed the ominously deep roots of the essence of modern technology in Western metaphysics. Concise and structured overviews of Heidegger's philosophy offer original and clarifying approaches to the major themes of Heidegger's work, with fresh and provocative perspectives on its significance for contemporary thinking and existence.

Cambridge Elements ☰

The Philosophy of Martin Heidegger

Elements in the Series

Heidegger on Being Affected
Katherine Withy

Heidegger on Eastern/Asian Thought
Lin Ma

Heidegger on Thinking
Lee Braver

Heidegger and Kierkegaard
George Pattison

Heidegger on Poetic Thinking
Charles Bambach

A full series listing is available at: www.cambridge.org/EPMH

Printed in the United States
by Baker & Taylor Publisher Services